7/10SB
4/14/5ᵛ
4/17 gk

322120

D0858669

Legends from Camp

POEMS BY LAWSON FUSAO INADA

COFFEE HOUSE PRESS :: MINNEAPOLIS :: 1992

Cover photo of the author with parents in Jerome Camp, Arkansas, c. 1943: photographer unknown. Camp photo c. 1944 by the author's uncle, Corporal Tom Saito, visiting on furlough. Fresno fish market photo of the author's uncle, Minoru Saito and Marcus Doi, c. 1939: photographer unknown. Photo of author with Mal Waldron: by Helga Motley. Oregon photo by Helga Motley. Performance photo by Hasato Baba. Back cover photo by Bill McClain.

The author wishes to thank the editors of the following magazines and newspapers where many of these poems first appeared: *Caliban, Chelsea, Fireweed, The Greenfield Review, International Examiner, Northwest Review, Open Places, Oregon English, Oregon Humanities, Pacific Citizen, Painted Hills Review,* and *The Seattle Review,*

The author wishes to thank the editors of the following anthologies where the following poems appeared: "My Father and Myself Facing the Sun" in *United States in Literature;* "Poems in Stone" in *Turning Shadows into Light;* "On Being Asian American" and "In/Vocation" in *The Big Aiiieeeee!;* "Turning it Over" in *Ergo!;* "John Coltrane" in *An Ear to the Ground;* "The Discovery of Tradition" in *The Big Aiiieeeee!* and *Leaving the Bough;* "Concentration Constellation" in *The Big Aiiieeeee!* and *Multiethnic Literature of the United States: Critical Introductions and Classroom Resources,* and "At the Stronghold" in *Califia.*

The publisher wishes to thank the following for their support of this project: the Minnesota State Arts Board; the Bush Foundation; the National Endowment for the Arts, a federal agency; and Northwest Area Foundation.

Coffee House Press books are available to stores through our primary distributor, Consortium Book Sales & Distribution, 287 East Sixth St., Suite 365, Saint Paul, MN 55101. Our books are also available through all major library distributors and jobbers and through most small press distributors including Bookpeople, Bookslinger, Inland, and Small Press Distribution.

For personal orders, catalogs or other information, write to:
Coffee House Press, 27 North Fourth Street, Minneapolis MN 55401.

Library of Congress Cataloging in Publication Data
Inada, Lawson Fusao.
    Legends from camp : poems / by Lawson Fusao Inada.
        p.   cm.
    ISBN 1-54489-004-7 : $11.95
    1. Japanese Americans—Evacuation and relocation, 1942-1945—Poetry.
    2. World War, 1939-1945—Japanese Americans—Poetry.
    3. Japanese Americans—Poetry. 4. Jazz musicians—Poetry.
    I. Title.
    PS3559.N3L43   1993
    811´.54Ädc20   92-38871, CIP

Contents

Oregon

Performance

Preface

It was a fresh, invigorating Indian summer morning in Phoenix, Oregon, where I was getting my car serviced—my transmission, actually. I went across the street to the steps of a pizza parlor to sit and wait. It was early, and business was just getting underway.

Suddenly, I heard sounds overhead—a couple of geese were calling, circling and calling. They circled and called for several minutes before getting underway, heading toward the mountains. And then they were gone. They left, but didn't leave—I could still see them, hear them, overhead in the sky of my mind. And as they called and flew, I felt a transmission from them—something passing, transmitted, from them to me in the form of thoughts and feelings. It was a wonder, a mystery—as geese and thoughts and feelings are—and I reached for my notebook and began to write, to follow where all that would lead me.

A poem emerged on the page: "A Couple of Geese Over Phoenix." A poem, yes, but also somewhat of a song, a meditation, and a painting—in about 200 words. That was it, that was enough; the poem emerged, happened, my transmission was serviced, and I was underway.

The point is: If it weren't for the geese, the feelings wouldn't have happened. And if it weren't for the poem, the thoughts and feelings would have stayed submerged, unexpresed, gradually fading and dispersing in my consciousness. And that would have been a shame—because those geese and that experience were worth sharing.

Such is the way, the gift, of this ancient and universal way known as poetry. Without it, and with the way our society is, I doubt that I could have shared the experience, really done justice to the geese and their messages. Instead, if I mentioned it at all in conversation, it would have become chit-chat and trivia: "Hey, guess what I saw today? Yup, boy, it was really something . . ."

Or, from another perspective, consider how I might have been described by a clerk in a store: "Hey, look at that guy out there! He's been sitting there for over an hour, writin' a letter or something . . ." "Well, I guess that's okay—as long as he's not in the way . . ."

The point is: Poetry happens—wherever, whenever it wants—and the poet simply has to be ready to follow through on the occasion. That's the way I do it, and it's always a wonder, a mystery, when it happens—something like a trance, a transmission, a "higher state" while sitting in the state you're in: you become a vehicle while awaiting your vehicle.

It's actually rather simple, ordinary, like the daydreams we all experience. Thus, it's no big deal—I just happen to write mine down, as poetry.

II

The poems in this book are arranged into sections—like chapters or movements—and each secion has an introduction. I wanted to provide background settings, contexts, for the poetry, in an informal, informative way. Enjoy.

Introduction

We went through a petrified forest to get there. Chunks of stone trees sprawled in the sand as we bumped and swayed slowly by. When we arrived at our destination, men on horseback topped a rise, coming down to greet us.

Where were we? Where was I? A summer camp, the Navajo Nation—brush arbors, corrals, sheep, horses—a high plateau, with mountains all around. Earlier that morning, I was passing through on asphalt when two women in traditional dress waved me down. Their truck had overheated; they needed a ride.

Sure, why not? As Agnes explained, they were getting supplies for "First Night"—the first of three nights, for a healing ceremony, a "sing." Each event would be held at a different site—in the mountains, and reached by horseback. I drove, they sang—a soft melody, over and over. Red earth, blue sky, petrified.

Grandmother was kneeling at the fire. She looked me over with her one good eye, then poured me coffee from an enamel pot. Children, adults, elders were seated all over—on rocks, on the ground, in shade and sun—chatting, laughing, eating . . .

They didn't pay me much mind, which was fine with me. After all, they had things to plan and do—things I knew nothing about. And it was a delicious feeling, actually (along with the delicious food—hot fry bread, steaming coffee, sizzling mutton), to be so ignorant in their midst, so I just sat there, enjoying the day, enjoying their way.

After a while, Grandmother said something to Agnes. "Grandmother asks who you are, where you're from." (Up to then, I was simply "Lawson from Oregon"—the driver with the foreign plates. They didn't pry, and neither did I. This question, though, was important.)

"Please tell her that my name is Inada, and that I am a Japanese from California." This got translated—perhaps the first time in the history of the world that "Inada" was spoken in Navajo—and Grandmother immediately replied, with something of a smirk, a smile, and a humph.

"Well, Grandmother says she doesn't know about all that. Grandmother says you're probably a Yazzie—maybe Delbert Yazzie's son, from up by Shiprock." I broke into a wide smile, and nodded—and Grandmother, smiling, nodded back. Then she continued.

"Grandmother says we would be honored to have you at First Night. And she also thanks you for giving us a ride." We nodded, smiled. "Please tell Grandmother thank you for the invitation and this wonderful food. The honor is mine."

Now, as far as I know, I'm still Fuzzy Inada's son, from Fresno. And because of that, I've been in many such similar situations—"tribal," with "clan" affiliations. I've been there all my life. I'll be there after death. Let me explain.

I've heard it said that the Japanese are "one big tribe." Well, I don't know about that—it's a convenient generalization—but for the sake of convenience I'll stay with the generalization, because I do know this much: wherever, whenever we may meet, or simply encounter one another, there's something in the air between us, a "spark of recognition" that might be termed a "tribal connection."

It runs deep, and is just there. It doesn't have to be mentioned. Call it kinship, if you will—something shared by "kindred spirits"—because, to me, it's more of a feeling than anything—like meeting a relative, or even meeting an ancestor. It runs deep—this sense of "our people."

It's also like "meeting yourself." And when you meet yourself, you belong. Which means that, while being an individual, you are also a crowd.

Now I don't want to get mystical here (or deal with the "Japanese mystique," whatever that's supposed to be); rather, what I'm talking about is "no big deal," just the way it is, and maybe it's the same for everybody. (Or could be; after all, we all stem from tribal societies.) No, we're common as clay, regular as rain; nothing exotic or special about us—and we just happen to have our own ways of keeping track, and "keeping with the times."

No big deal, actually. Just history, pure and simple—lineage, legacy. It simply comes with the territory—and if you don't like it, you can do something about it. For instance, one of my students told me: "Yeah, you might say I'm a Japanese American, but back home in Idaho I'm just your basic redneck cowboy." Okay, good enough, dude. Or, from another student: "Yes, I am a woman from Japan, but I think of myself as an artist first—and from here I will go to Spain, to study painting." All right—go for it!

IV

Myself, I'll admit—I haven't always liked being Japanese, and there are some Japanese I don't necessarily like. No big deal, as I said. I've learned to live with it, even work at it—by reading about a country where I've never been—and I'm often surprised by how Japanese I really am: "Hello, I'm calling to inquire about your academic . . ." "Are you Japanese?" "Well, uh, sure. Are you?" "Yup. Now what did you want to know about . . ." "Hey, wait a minute, lady! Who are you? Where are you from?"

And then we're off and running—the customary procedure of sharing "tribal" and "clan" affiliations, and so on down the line . . . "No kidding? I'll be darned."

Let me do the same for you. A simple show-and-tell procedure—some places, some dates. Do with it what you will. And for the sake of convenience, let's just go back a ways to the petrified forest.

Dusk. Little summer breeze. Full moon rising. Stars. Birds, insects. Scent of juniper, sage. Sand, earth. Way over there, in the mountains—maybe that's the First Night campfire. Let's proceed—striking "sparks of recognition."

For starters, let's say these rocks over here are Japan. Close enough. My mother's clan, Saito, comes from, and is still in, Wakayama Prefecture, on the main island, not all that far, "walking distance," from Osaka and Kyoto—which means that her parents had a semi-urban experience, at least for the 19th century. This other rock is the island of Kyushu, the southland, my father's clan being from Kumamoto Prefecture—the "sticks." (Or the "fields"—since "Inada" means "Rice-field." You get the picture.)

Prefecture-of-origin is very important to us—causing nods of recognition, acknowledgment—because the "lay of the land" says something about who and how we are, in Japan or elsewhere. As a matter of fact, I could stop right here, at these rocks, because they have my history and destiny written all over them.

But let's go over here, to America. (Down there, of course, is South America—where there's more of us than here. And naturally enough, my Brazilian clans speak Portuguese. And these little rocks are Hawaii—where my Inada grandfather labored on a plantation, for passage to the mainland.)

More "islands," right—this big flat one being Fresno (urban/Saito/Fresno Fish Market, mother born in back of the store, 1912), and this big bumpy one being the greater San Jose region (rural/Inada/share-croppers, father born on the Pajaro River, Watsonville, 1910). These "islands/prefectures" are also very important (more nods), and my father is the "chief" of Fresno's Kumamoto Prefecture Association. Moreover, my clans and extended clans are prominent in both places.

This is where I come in—Fresno, 1938. Not just a place, not just a date, and I'm not just a Sansei (third-generation), either. Rather, I'm an "older" Sansei, or a "pre-war" Sansei—and once again, we could stop right here, because the facts of my birth say just about everything about me: history, destiny, character, personality, the whole prophecy.

Which is to say: I speak Japanese, have a Japanese name, and was in the camps. Moonlight isn't necessary to see, and feel, the meaning. It's written all over me, wherever I am.

And with the camps came, sure enough, more "islands," and what might be termed "re-tribalization"—and I'd say living in a specific place with a related people constitutes "tribal" life. And with the camps came extremely significant designations and distinctions that are with us to this very day: "What camp were you in?" Or, as my great-grand-children in the next century will say: "What camp were they in?"

In my case, my lineage and legacy includes three—and each camp was different, and the same. So let's see—where were we? Well, back over there, that's the Fresno Assembly Center, the county fair-grounds—an "instant" camp, a "pre-camp" camp, with an instant leg-acy. Now over there—that low-lying rock in the brush—that's Jerome Camp, in the Mississippi Delta, the swamp of Arkansas. Right—clear over there.

And this smooth one where we're standing—with the sand on it, see?—is Amache Camp, in the Colorado desert, not all that far from here. While we're at it, let's let that little stone by your foot stand for Leupp—a "mini-camp" right here on the Navajo Nation. (And, yes, we had major camps on other reservations; so you might say that it makes sense that the chief camps administrator went on to become chief of the Bureau of Indian Affairs, where he "re-deployed" his policy of "relocation." Which included, yes, "termination." Which reminds me—down the ridge, in Europe, our relatives had base camps in Italy, France, Germany, and some of them liberated a camp called Dachau.)

Well, enough of that. Speak your piece, if you want. These rocks aren't going anywhere. Otherwise, we can just mosey on down to camp—or maybe even, whoa, saddle up and head to First Night. Follow the fire, you know—those "sparks of recognition."

Boy—listen to those coyotes! But you know—I've had this feeling all along: We are not alone.

—Lawson Fusao Inada

For Janet, Miles, Lowell,
and
Masako and Fusaji Inada

SECTION I

Camp

Camp

"Hello, Lawson? This is President Roosevelt speaking. Now, as you may know, son, we're at war with Japan, so I'm going to have to put you and your family in camp." That phone call never came, but the effect was the same. And three years later, when the president died, we were still in camp.

We've lived with the experience since—on a continual basis. And I've often wondered: What does it all mean? History offers clues: The *American* camps are part of the American experience, with many patterns and connections; also, there are international ramifications to consider, going back at least to President Fillmore in 1854, and the "opening" of Japan. (Actually, Columbus was heading to "Cipaugu," Japan.)

Still there's a remoteness to history, and to simply know the facts is not always satisfactory. There's more to life than that. So you might say I've taken matters into my own hands—taken the camp experience in my hands, stood in the sun, and held it up to the light.

What did I find? What I *expected* to find: Aspects of humanity, the human condition.

Presidio of San Francisco, California
May 3, 1942

INSTRUCTIONS
TO ALL PERSONS OF
JAPANESE
ANCESTRY
Living in the Following Area:

All of that portion of the City of Los Angeles, State of California, within that boundary beginning at the point at which North Figueroa Street meets a line following the middle of the Los Angeles River; thence southerly and following the said line to East First Street; thence westerly on East First Street to Alameda Street; thence southerly on Alameda Street to East Third Street; thence northwesterly on East Third Street to Main Street; thence northerly on Main Street to First Street; thence northwesterly on First Street to Figueroa Street; thence northeasterly on Figueroa Street to the point of beginning.

Pursuant to the provisions of Civilian Exclusion Order No. 33, this Headquarters, dated May 3, 1942, all persons of Japanese ancestry, both alien and non-alien, will be evacuated from the above area by 12 o'clock noon, P. W. T., Saturday, May 9, 1942.

No Japanese person living in the above area will be permitted to change residence after 12 o'clock noon, P. W. T., Sunday, May 3, 1942, without obtaining special permission from the representative of the Commanding General, Southern California Sector, at the Civil Control Station located at:

Japanese Union Church,
120 North San Pedro Street,
Los Angeles, California.

Such permits will only be granted for the purpose of uniting members of a family, or in cases of grave emergency.

The Civil Control Station is equipped to assist the Japanese population affected by this evacuation in the following ways:

1. Give advice and instructions on the evacuation.
2. Provide services with respect to the management, leasing, sale, storage or other disposition of most kinds of property, such as real estate, business and professional equipment, household goods, boats, automobiles and livestock.
3. Provide temporary residence elsewhere for all Japanese in family groups.
4. Transport persons and a limited amount of clothing and equipment to their new residence.

The Following Instructions Must Be Observed:

1. A responsible member of each family, preferably the head of the family, or the person in whose name most of the property is held, and each individual living alone, will report to the Civil Control Station to receive further instructions. This must be done between 8:00 A. M. and 5:00 P. M. on Monday, May 4, 1942, or between 8:00 A. M. and 5:00 P. M. on Tuesday, May 5, 1942.
2. Evacuees must carry with them on departure for the Assembly Center, the following property:
   (a) Bedding and linens (no mattress) for each member of the family;
   (b) Toilet articles for each member of the family;
   (c) Extra clothing for each member of the family;
   (d) Sufficient knives, forks, spoons, plates, bowls and cups for each member of the family;
   (e) Essential personal effects for each member of the family.

All items carried will be securely packaged, tied and plainly marked with the name of the owner and numbered in accordance with instructions obtained at the Civil Control Station. The size and number of packages is limited to that which can be carried by the individual or family group.

3. No pets of any kind will be permitted.
4. No personal items and no household goods will be shipped to the Assembly Center.
5. The United States Government through its agencies will provide for the storage, at the sole risk of the owner, of the more substantial household items, such as iceboxes, washing machines, pianos and other heavy furniture. Cooking utensils and other small items will be accepted for storage if crated, packed and plainly marked with the name and address of the owner. Only one name and address will be used by a given family.
6. Each family, and individual living alone, will be furnished transportation to the Assembly Center or will be authorized to travel by private automobile in a supervised group. All instructions pertaining to the movement will be obtained at the Civil Control Station.

Go to the Civil Control Station between the hours of 8:00 A.M. and 5:00 P.M., Monday, May 4, 1942, or between the hours of 8:00 A.M. and 5:00 P.M., Tuesday, May 5, 1942, to receive further instructions.

J. L. DeWITT
Lieutenant General, U. S. Army
Commanding

SEE CIVILIAN EXCLUSION ORDER NO. 33.

Instructions to All Persons

Let us take
what we can
for the occasion:

>   Ancestry. *(Ancestry)*
>   All of that portion. *(Portion)*
>   With the boundary. *(Boundary)*
>   Beginning. *(Beginning)*
>   At the point. *(Point)*
>   Meets a line. *(Line)*
>   Following the middle. *(Middle)*
>   Thence southerly. *(Southerly)*
>   Following the said line. *(Following) (Said)*
>   Thence westerly. *(Westerly)*
>   Thence northerly. *(Northerly)*
>   To the point. *(Point)*
>   Of beginning. *(Beginning) (Ancestry)*

Let us bring
what we need
for the meeting:

>   Provisions. *(Provisions)*
>   Permission. *(Permission)*
>   Commanding. *(Commanding)*
>   Uniting. *(Uniting)*
>   Family. *(Family)*

Let us have
what we have
for the gathering:

>   Civil. *(Civil)*
>   Ways. *(Ways)*
>   Services. *(Services)*

Respect. *(Respect)*
Management. *(Management)*
Kinds. *(Kinds)*
Goods. *(Goods)*
For all. *(All)*

Let us take
what we can
for the occasion:

Responsible.

Individual.

Sufficient.

Personal.

Securely.

Civil.

Substantial.

Accepted.

Given.

Authorized.

Let there be
Order.

Let us be
Wise.

Legends from Camp

It began as truth, as fact.
That is, at least the numbers, the statistics,
are there for verification:

10 camps, 7 state,
120,113 residents.

Still, figures can lie: people are born, die.
And as for the names of the places themselves,
these, too, were subject to change:

Denson or Jerome, Arkansas;
Gila or Canal, Arizona;
Tule Lake or Newell, California;
Amache or Granada, Colorado.

As was the War Relocation Authority
with its mention of "camps" or "centers" for:

Assembly,
Concentration,
Detention,
Evacuation,
Internment,
Relocation,—
among others.

"Among others"—that's important also. Therefore, let's not forget contractors, carpenters, plumbers, electricians and architects, sewage engineers, and all the untold thousands who provided the materials, decisions, energy, and transportation to make the camps a success, including, of course, the administrators, clerks, and families who not only swelled the population but were there to make and keep things shipshape according to D.C. directives and people deploying coffee in the various offices of the WRA, overlooking, overseeing rivers, cityscapes, bays, whereas in actual camp the troops—excluding, of course, our aunts and uncles and sisters and brothers and fathers and mothers serving stateside, in the South Pacific, the European theater—pretty much had things in order; finally, there were the grandparents, who since the turn of the century, simply assumed they were living in America "among others."

The situation, obviously, was rather confusing.
It obviously confused simple people
who had simply assumed they were friends, neighbors,
colleagues, partners, patients, customers, students,
teachers, of, not so much "aliens" or "non-aliens,"
but likewise simple, unassuming people
who paid taxes as fellow citizens and populated
pews and desks and fields and places
of ordinary American society and commerce.

Rumors flew. Landed. What's what? Who's next?

And then, "just like that," it happened.
And then, "just like that," it was over.
Sun, moon, stars—they came, and went.

And then, and then, things happened,
and as they ended they kept happening,
and as they happened they ended
and began again, happening, happening,

until the event, the experience, the history,
slowly began to lose its memory,
gradually drifting into a kind of fiction—

a "true story based on fact,"
but nevertheless with "all the elements of fiction"—
and then, and then, sun, moon, stars,
we come, we come, to where we are:
Legend.

I. THE LEGEND OF PEARL HARBOR

"Aloha or Bust!"

We got here first!

II. THE LEGEND OF THE HUMANE SOCIETY

This is as
simple
as it gets:

In a pinch,
dispose
of your pets.

III. THE LEGEND OF PROTEST

The F.B.I. swooped in early,
taking our elders in the process—

for "subversive" that and this.

People ask: "Why didn't you protest?"
Well, you might say: "They had *hostages*."

IV. THE LEGEND OF LOST BOY

Lost Boy was not his name.

He had another name, a given name—
at another, given time and place—
but those were taken away.

The road was taken away.
The dog was taken away.
The food was taken away.
The house was taken away.

The boy was taken away—
but he was not lost.
Oh, no—he knew exactly where he was—

and if someone had asked
or needed directions,
he could have told them:

"This is the fairgrounds.
That's Ventura Avenue over there.
See those buildings? That's town!"

This place also had buildings—
but they were all black, the same.
There were no houses, no trees,
no hedges, no streets, no homes.

But, every afternoon, a big truck
came rolling down the rows.
It was full of water, cool,
and the boy would follow it, cool.
It smelled like rain,
and even made some rainbows!

So on this hot, hot day,
the boy followed and followed,
and when the truck stopped,
then sped off in the dust,
the boy didn't know where he was.

He knew, but he didn't know
which barrack was what.
And so he cried. A lot.
He looked like the truck.

Until Old Man Ikeda
found him, bawled him out.
Until Old Man Ikeda
laughed and called him
"Lost Boy."
Until Old Man Ikeda
walked him through
the rows, and rows,
the people, the people,
the crowd.

Until his mother
cried and laughed
and called him
"Lost Boy."

Until Lost Boy
thought he was found.

V. THE LEGEND OF FLYING BOY

This only happened once,
but once is enough—
so listen carefully.

There was a boy
who had nothing to do.
No toys, no nothing.
Plus, it was hot
in the empty room.

Well, the room was full
of sleeping parents
and an empty cot.

The boy was bored.
He needed something to do.
A hairpin on the floor
needed picking up.

It, too, needed
something to do—
like the wire, the socket
over there on the wall.

You know the rest
of the story—
but not the best
of the story:

the feel of power,
the empowering act
of being the air!

You had to be there.
Including the activity
that followed.

Flying Boy—
where are you?

Flying Boy—
you flew!

VI. THE LEGEND OF THE GREAT ESCAPE

The people were passive:
Even when a train paused
in the Great Plains, even
when soldiers were eating,
they didn't try to escape.

VII. THE LEGEND OF TALKS-WITH-HANDS

Actually, this was a whole,
intact family who lived
way over there at the edge
of our Arkansas camp.

Their name? I don't know.
Ask my mother—such ladies
were friends from "church camp."

Also, the family didn't just
talk with their hands.
The man made toys with his,
the woman knitted, and the boy
could fold his paper airplanes.

And, back in those days,
a smile could go a long ways
toward saying something.

And we were all ears.
Talking, and during prayers.

VIII. THE LEGEND OF THE HAKUJIN WOMAN

This legend is about legendary
freedom of choice, options—

because this Hakujin woman
chose to be there.

She could have been anywhere—
New York City, Fresno, or over

with the administration.
Instead, she selected an ordinary

barracks room to share
with her husband.

IX. THE LEGEND OF COYOTE

Buddy was his name. And, yes, he was a Trickster.
He claimed he wasn't even one of us.
He claimed he had some kind of "tribe" somewhere.

He claimed he "talked with spirits."
He claimed he could "see God in the stars."
He claimed the "spirits are everywhere."

He was just a kid. We were just barracks neighbors.
And the one thing Buddy did was make paper airplanes
out of any catalog page or major announcement—

and I mean to tell you, those things could fly!
Those things would go zipping off over barbed wire,
swirl by amazed soldiers in guard towers,

and, sometimes in the swamp, they didn't seem to land.
That was when another claim came in—they went
"all the way to Alaska" and also "back to the tribe."

Buddy. If I had smarts like that, I'd be an engineer.
Buddy. His dreams, his visions. He simply disappeared.

My uncle was going overseas.
He was heading to the European theater,
and we were all going to miss him.

He had been stationed by Cheyenne,
and when he came to say good-bye
he brought me a little bag of marbles.

But the best one, an agate, cracked.
It just broke, like bone, like flesh—
so my uncle comforted me with this story:

> *"When we get home to Fresno,*
> *I will take you into the basement*
> *and give you my box of magic marbles.*
>
> *These marbles are marbles—*
> *so they can break and crack and chip—*
> *but they are also magic*
>
> *so they can always be fixed:*
> *all you have to do is leave them*
> *overnight in a can of Crisco*
>
> *next day they're good as new."*

Uncle. Uncle. Uncle. What happened to *you?*

XI. THE LEGEND OF SHOYU

Legend had it that, even in Arkansas,
some people had soy sauce.
Well, not exactly *our* soy sauce,
which we were starved for,
but some related kind of dark
and definitive liquid
to flavor you through the day.

That camp was in the Delta,
where the Muddy Waters lay.

Black shoyu. Black shoyu.
Let me taste the blues!

XII. THE LEGEND OF THE JEROME SMOKESTACK

There is no legend.
It just stands there
in a grassy field,
the brush of swampland,
soaring up to the sky.

It's just the tallest
thing around for miles.
Pilots fly by it.

Some might say it's
a tribute, a monument,
a memorial to something.
But no, not really.

It's just a massive
stack of skills, labor,
a multitude of bricks.

And what it expressed
was exhaust, and waste.

It's just a pile of past.
Home of the wind, rain,
residence of bodies, nests.
I suppose it even sings.

But no, it's not legend.
It just stands, withstands.

XIII. THE LEGEND OF BAD BOY

Bad Boy wasn't his name.
And as a matter of fact,
there were a lot of them.

Bad Boy watched. He saw
soldiers shoot rats, snakes;
they even shot a dog.

Bad Boy learned. He did
what he could to insects—
whatever it took to be a Man.

XIV. THE LEGEND OF GOOD GIRL

Good Girl was good. She really was.
She never complained; she helped others.
She worked hard; she played until tired.
Good Girl, as you guessed, was Grandmother.

XV. THE LEGEND OF THE FULL MOON OVER AMACHE

As it turned out,
Amache is said to have been named
for an Indian princess—

not a regular squaw—

who perished upstream,
in the draw,
of the Sand Creek Massacre.

Her bones floated down
to where the camp was now.

The full moon?
It doesn't have anything to do
with this. It's just there,

illuminating, is all.

XVI. THE LEGEND OF AMATERASU

The Sun Goddess ruled the Plain of Heaven.
She did this for eons and eons, forever
and ever, before anyone could remember.

Amaterasu, as a Goddess, could always do
exactly as She wanted; thus, She haunted
Colorado like the myth She was, causing

wrinkles in the heat, always watching You.

Hey, come on now, let's hear it for Groucho!
Groucho was a florist by profession
and the doggone best natural-born comedian.

It was said by some, with tears in their eyes,
that ol' Groucho could make a delivery to a funeral
and have everyone just a-rollin' in the aisles.

Even on the worst of bad days, he was worth a smile.

Groucho was Groucho—before, during, after.
Wherever he was, there was bound to be laughter.

And the thing is, he really wasn't all that witty.
He was actually serious, which made it really funny—

him and that broken English and the gimpy leg.
He was a reserved bachelor too, a devoted son
who sent whatever he had to his mother in Japan.

Still, he had that something that tickled people
pink and red and white and blue and even had
the lizards lapping it up, basking in it, happy!

Maybe that was the magic—he was "seriously happy."
And not only legend has it, but I was there,
when a whole mess of pheasants came trekking clear
from Denver, just for Groucho and the heck of it,
and proceeded to make themselves into sukiyaki—

with the rest of us yukking and yakking it up all the while!

Ah, yes, Groucho! He brought joy out in people!
And when he finally got back home to Sacramento
and the news, he threw his flowers in the air,

toward Hiroshima—and of course he died laughing!

Superman, being Superman,
had his headquarters out there
somewhere between Gotham City
and Battle Creek, Michigan.

Superman, being Superman,
even knew my address:

> Block 6G , 5 C
> Amache, Colorado
> America

And Superman, being Superman,
sent me his Secret Code,
based on all the Planets—

with explicit instructions
to keep it hidden from others,
like "under a bed, a sofa,
or under stockings in a drawer."

Superman, being Superman,
didn't seem to understand.
Where could anything hide?

And, since we all spoke code
on a regular basis, day to day,

Superman, being Superman,
gathered up his Planets
and simply flew away!

XIX. THE LEGEND OF OTHER CAMPS

They were out there, all right,
but nobody knew what they were up to.
It was tough enough deciphering
what was going on right here.

Still, even barracks have ears:
so-and-so shot and killed;
so-and-so shot and lived;
infants, elders, dying of heat;
epidemics, with so little care.

It was tough enough deciphering
what was going on anywhere.

XX. THE LEGEND OF HOME

Home, too, was out there.
It had names like
Marysville, Placerville,
Watsonville, and Lodi—

and they were all big cities
or at least bigger than camp.

And they were full of trees,
and grass, with fruit
for the picking, dogs
to chase, cats to catch

on streets and roads
where Joey and Judy lived.

Imagine that!
The blue tricycle
left in the weeds somewhere!

And when you came to a fence,
you went around it!

And one of those homes
not only had a tunnel
but an overpass
that, when you went over,

revealed everything
going on forever up to
a gleaming bridge
leading into neon lights
and ice cream leaning
double-decker.

Imagine that!

XXI. THE LEGEND OF THE BLOCK 6G OBAKE

I still don't mention his name in public.
And I'm sure he's long since passed on.
As a matter of fact, he may have died in camp.

He was that old. And he was also slow—
slow and loud enough to frighten
grown men out of their wits.

And all he did was go around our block
banging a stick on a garbage can lid
and chanting, droning, *Block 6G Obake.*"

He did that every evening, when the ghost
to him appeared—his personal ghost,
or whatever it was that haunted the camp.

He was punctual, persistent, specific.
And then I guess he either moved or died.
Whatever it was, we never spoke of him.

Because, the thing is, he was right.
Amache really was haunted. As it still is.
Amache was, is, are: Nightly, on television.

XXII. THE LEGEND OF BURNING THE WORLD

It got so cold in Colorado we would burn the world.
That is, the rocks, the coal, that trucks would dump in a pile.
Come on, children! Everybody! Bundle up! Let's go!
But then, in the warmth, you remembered how everything goes up
In smoke.

XXIII. THE LEGEND OF TARGETS

It got so hot in Colorado we would start to go crazy.
This included, of course, soldiers in uniform, on patrol.
So, once a week, just for relief, they went out for target practice.
We could hear them shooting hundreds of rounds, shouting
    like crazy.
It sounded like a New Year's celebration! Such fun is not to
    be missed!
So someone cut a deal, just for the kids, and we went out past the
    fence.
The soldiers shot, and between rounds, we dug in the dunes for
    bullets.
It was great fun! They would aim at us, go *"Pow!"* and we'd
    shout *"Missed!"*

XXIV. THE LEGEND OF BUDDHA

Buddha said we are all buddhas.

XXV. THE LEGEND OF LEAVING

Let's have one more turn
around the barracks.
Let's have one more go
down the rows, rows, rows.
Let's have one last chance
at the length of the fence—

slow, slow, slow,
dust, dust, dust,
billowing behind
the emperor's caravan,
king of the walled city.

Head of State.
Head of Fence.
Head of Towers.
Head of Gate.

Length, height, weight,
corners and corrections
duly dedicated
to my dimensions
and directions.

It's early, it's late.
I'm in no hurry.
An Amache evening.
an Amache morning.
Slowly, this date
came dusty, approaching.

One more turn,
another go,
one last chance—

fast and slow—-
before I go.

Who would have known.
Who would have guessed
the twists, the turn
of such events
combined in this
calligraphy of echoes
as inevitable,
as inscrutable
as nostalgia

jangling the nerves,
jangling the keys
of my own release.
Let's have one more turn
of the lock, the key.
Let's have one last look
as I leave
this morning, evening.

All my belongings
are gathered.
All my connections
are scattered.

What's over the horizon?
What's left to abandon?
What's left to administer?
Will anyone ever need
another Camp Director?

Poems from Amache Camp

I.

"Dear Lawson,

    2 Ys U R,
    2 Ys U B,
    I C U R
    2 Ys 4 Me!

        Your friend,

        Bobby"

II.

"Dear Lawson,

    I meet you early,
    I meet you late,
    I meet you at
    Amache Gate!

        Always,

        Naomi"

Concentration Constellation

In this earthly configuration,
we have, not points of light,
but prominent barbs of dark.

It's all right there on the map.
It's all right there in the mind.
Find it. If you care to look.

Begin between the Golden State's
highest and lowest elevations
and name that location

Manzanar. Rattlesnake a line
southward to the zone
of Arizona, to the home
of natives on the reservation,
and call those *Gila, Poston*.

Then just take your time
winding your way across
the Southwest expanse, the Lone
Star State of Texas, gathering
up a mess of blues as you
meander around the banks
of the humid Mississippi; yes,
just make yourself at home
in the swamps of Arkansas,
for this is *Rohwer* and *Jerome*.

By now, you weary of the way.
It's a big country, you say.
It's a big history, hardly
halfway though—with *Amache*
looming in the Colorado desert,
Heart Mountain high in wide

Wyoming, *Minidoka* on the moon
of Idaho, then down to Utah's
jewel of *Topaz* before finding
yourself at northern California's
frozen shore of *Tule Lake* . . .

Now regard what sort of shape
this constellation takes.
It sits there like a jagged scar,
massive, on the massive landscape.
It lies there like the rusted wire
of a twisted and remembered fence.

Looking Back at Camp

To get into the fair,
You have to pay admission.

We got in for free,
To the Fresno Family Prison.

II. JEROME CAMP

Every so often,
I sit down with
a neighbor.

I sit and listen
as he plays
the guitar.

He sings of love,
of luck, of want,
whatever he dares.

What he doesn't
sing about is
what's over there —

guard towers, guns,
big cabins beyond
the plantation.

Or, at night,
how searchlights
find us here.

And then he sings,
soft and low,
about Chicago.

III. AMACHE CAMP

I work on campus.
I try to concentrate.

Still, things sneak
up to remind me:

"This is *not* Amache!"

SECTION II

Fresno

Fresno

I.

> "Fresno, California's eighth largest city, is the financial headquarters for San Joaquin Valley agribusiness. Its roots are firmly planted in the rich soil of history, which makes for an interesting visit."
> —Robertson McCarta, *California*

> "Fresno's population was one-half foreign-born. It was reported that forty-eight different nationalities had children in the city's schools. The Southern Pacific Railroad tracks constituted a racial 'pale', with the immigrants and dark-skinned groups living mainly on the west side of the tracks; the Armenians were the first to break through the barrier."   —Anne Loftis, *California: Where the Twain Did Meet*

Fresno. What does it mean? What is the meaning of Fresno? Well, Fresno means "ash tree" in Spanish. There is also some sort of wheeled contraption used in highway contruction called a "Fresno." Or, for tourists, Fresno is a place in the "middle of nowhere," a place to go through on the way to somewhere— San Francisco, Los Angeles, Yosemite, Kings Canyon, Sequoia National Park.

Fresno depends on who you ask, who you are. And Fresno doesn't mean much. Unless you happen to be of Armenian, Chinese, Japanese, Pilipino ancestry. Unless you happen to be Hmong—and 30,000 Hmong moved there recently. Unless you happen to be German, Italian. Unless you happen to be Chicano, African American, an Okie—then Fresno rings bells in your family. Unless you happen to be one of many "people of the land."

And the land around Fresno is the "richest agricultural area on the face of the earth." So the next time you sit down at the table, ask yourself: "Did this come from *Fresno?*"

II.

"Fresno's other downtown seems to lie along Fresno and Tulare streets, right near the freeway. It's got a dense mixture of Chinese, Japanese, and Mexican restaurants, most of them pretty rugged-looking. Be bold, or choose one of the safe-looking, never places. . . .You won't go far before you bump into the Fresno Buddhist Temple."

—Neal Weiner, *The Interstate Gourmet*

"My grandmother Lucy and her daughter Takoohi used to send me to the Fresno Fish Market in Chinatown sixty years ago."

—William Saroyan, *Obituaries*

Saroyan is the foremost Fresno writer—Pulitzer-Prize winner, world traveler. Still, he came home to die in Fresno. Which says a great deal about him, and Fresno. And there are deep connections between us. We only met once, but he was gracious enough to contribute a statement for the cover of my first book, and before that, in the 1940s, he contributed the Introduction, and his considerable prestige, to the first book of fiction by a Japanese American, Toshio Mori's *Yokohama, California*. Mori and Saroyan were friends, Mori and I were friends, and in 1985 I wrote the new Introduction to that book.

But our connections run deeper than the literary. Since Saroyan frequented the Fresno Fish Market, he had to know my family— particularly my grandparents, who founded that market in 1912, Fresno's first fish store, an institution for seventy years. My mother was born there, in Jap Alley, a block from China Alley. And Saroyan is right in calling the area "Chinatown."

That's what we called it— the business district of the greater West Side. That's what it had always been called, I suppose, by the generic folks who settled the "regular" Fresno, "un-Chinatown." I don't know what the Chinese called it. Probably "Home." Or, having survived what they did, with their traditions intact, they might have dubbed it "The Benevolent Kingdom Bordering the Silver Rails We Laid."

Whatever, the people staked a claim, and meant to defend it. Call it what you will, buster. Have a looksee. Chow down. But we've got you covered. Thus, the pattern of survival, of toughness, was set—and continues to this day.

Then other folks moved in—other immigrants, other coloreds,—making "Chinatown" a misnomer, but "Chinatown" it remains. With many "remains" to be found, since China Alley itself is no more.

But the West Side is still there—going strong, in full force. On the surface, it appears to be a "colonized country" with a Third World population; or on the outskirts, amidst the vineyards and cottonfields, you might think you were in the Deep South or northern Guatemala. It's tough out there; it's tough in the housing projects; it's tough all over the West Side— and you have to have your resources in order.

Thus, the proliferation of all the places of worship—from houses to storefronts to temples, mosques, churches. Because, above all, and deep beneath, the West Side is a most *soulful* place: rooted in racism, watered by want, the *spirit thrives!*

To Get to Fresno

To get to Fresno,
you need to turn left
in New York City.

To get to Fresno,
you need to
pop a U-turn
in Tucson.

To get to Fresno,
you need to go up to people
in the marketplace
in Lima, Peru,
and just say "Fresno"
several times.

They'll give you directions,
but be sure you don't settle for
Fresnillo, Mexico—
because you want
the *Real Thing:*

    Fresno, California,
      West Coast,
      U. S. of A.

To get to Fresno,
you have to be
dancing in Zimbabwe
and ask some people
through the music and the heat;

They won't lose the beat,
and from there you can
dance back to Fresno.

To get to Fresno,
you have to go
around and around
the traffic circle
in Berlin, Germany,
around and around
some historical statue
and after you get tired of that
you have to tell some policeman
that it's *Fresno* you're after—
not Paris, not London,
certainly not Rome,

but over there, you know,
beyond all that,
beyond the ocean,
both continents,
and over to F Street, you know,
and the old fish store.

To get to Fresno,
you have to get into, somehow,
the Golden Arches of Moscow,
where they'll tell you to
make a right
at the Ukraine K-Mart
and keep on a-going.

To get to Fresno,
you have to walk along the Ganges
at dusk,
and then just wade in up to your waist,
soaking your robe
as you recite
"Fresno Fresno Fresno"
over and over,

and from there, really,
any direction will get you to Fresno.

To get to Fresno,
you have to look at your watch
at the edge of the Bering Sea,
overlooking the ice floe;
your watch is set
to Fresno time,
so you wave good-bye
to whales, polar bears, seals,

and set out
south through the tundra.

To get to Fresno,
you have to know
where you're getting,

you have to know
what you're getting.

To get to Fresno,
you have to
live in Fresno,

you have to
be in Fresno
for a long time;

you have to
drive all around Fresno
over and over;

you have to
walk all around Fresno
through all the seasons;

you have to
talk about Fresno,
think about Fresno,

ask about Fresno,
know about Fresno;

and just about the time
you think you're
familiar with Fresno,

think that you
finally know Fresno,
really know Fresno,
the *real* Fresno,

someone will ask you,
or you will ask yourself:

> "*Where* is Fresno?"
> "*Who* is Fresno?"
> "*What* is Fresno?"

and despite all of your knowledge,
all of your maps,
all of your facts—

all the certificates and documents
and photographs
you have as proof—

Fresno, as you *think* you know it,
Fresno, as you *know* you know it,

this it, this thing, this place
called "Fresno"

will disappear before your very eyes,

gone forever,
as if it never
existed—

and when you blink your eyes again,
you will be standing in line
or driving through traffic,

startled back to your senses,
to life as you know it, accept it,

and say to yourself:

> *"Welcome back, Fresno.*
> *Welcome back home."*

Finding the Center

Charles and I had played there all along.
It was dirt. Good dirt. It made good
gardens—tomatoes, squash, peppers, corn.
It made good mud. It made good mounds
around the orange tree, the cactus,
for rivers and roads and boats and cars
living life in the valleys and mountains.

That was about it, for now—
Mama Gomez was calling us in for supper—
but tonight, if we were good, or lucky,
she would feed us sweet tortillas
and the crunchiest iced tea
as we sat on the porch, watching
moths meet the moon, fluttering stars,
and whatever else was doing on C Street.

Yes, it was a good life, on good dirt—
dirt to be smoothed over for marbles
mañana, and as we worked the earth
for our bright little spheres,
we looked for all the world like farmers.
Two kids, neighbors, an industrious lot.

This is why it didn't surprise us
when the dirt was finally discovered.
And, oh, the attention it got.
It was even, as they say, "in the paper"—
politicians and surveyors going loco,
placing a plaque in the Gomez yard.

And what the plaque said, we already knew.
It was obvious, and if they had asked
me or Charles or the Gomez family,
we could have saved them a lot of money:

"You're standing on it:
This dirt
Is the exact
Geographical
Center
Of the State
of
California!"

Rayford's Song

Rayford's song was Rayford's song,
but it was not his alone, to own.

He had it, though, and kept it to himself
as we rowed-rowed-rowed the boat
through English country gardens
with all the whispering hope
we could muster, along with occasional
choruses of funiculi-funicula!

Weren't we a cheery lot—
comin' 'round the mountain
with Susanna, banjos on our knees,
rompin' through the leaves
of the third-grade music textbook.

Then Rayford Butler raised his hand.
For the first time, actually,
in all the weeks he had been in class,
and for the only time before he'd leave.
Yes, quiet Rayford, silent Rayford,
little Rayford, dark Rayford—
always in the same overalls—
that Rayford, Rayford Butler, raised his hand:

>   "Miss Gordon, ma'am—
>   we always singing your songs.
>   Could I sing one of my own?"

Pause. We looked at one another;
we looked at Rayford Butler;
we looked up at Miss Gordon, who said:

>   "Well, I suppose so, Rayford—
>   if you insist. Go ahead.
>   Just one song. Make it short."

And Rayford Butler stood up very straight,
and in his high voice, sang:

> *"Suh-whing ah-loooow,*
> *suh-wheeet ah-charr-eee-oohh,*
> *ah-comin' for to carr-eee*
> *meee ah-hooooome . . ."*

Pause. Classroom, school, schoolyard,
neighborhood, the whole world
focusing on that one song, one voice
which had a light to it, making even
Miss Gordon's white hair shine
in the glory of it, glowing
in the radiance of the song.

Pause. Rayford Butler sat down.
And while the rest of us
may have been spellbound,
on Miss Gordon's face
was something like a smile,
or perhaps a frown:

> "Very good, Rayford.
> However, I must correct you:
> the word is 'chari*ot.*'
> 'Chari*ot.*' And there is no
> such thing as a 'chari*o.*'
> Do you understand me?"

> "But Miss Gordon . . ."

> "I said 'chari*ot,* chari*ot.*'
> Can you pronounce that for me?"

> "Yes, Miss Gordon. Chari*ot.*"

"Very good, Rayford.
Now, class, before we return
to our book, would anyone else
care to sing a song of their own?"

Our songs, our songs, were there—
on tips of tongues, but stuck
in throats— songs of love,
fun, animals, and valor, songs
of other lands, in other languages,
but they just wouldn't come out.
Where did our voices go?

Rayford's song was Rayford's song,
but it was not his alone, to own.

"Well, then, class—
let's turn our books to
'Old Black Joe.'"

Sweaty

For Herbert and Henry Palomino

West Fresno is the only place I know
where "sweaty" is a term of praise.

"Sweaty" this, and "sweaty" that—
and you really had or were something—

money, job, car, style, clothes . . .
I've got some of that, I suppose—

so some might say I'm "sweaty."
If not, I'm ready. I aspire

to perspire in some *sweaty* poems!

Listening to Hmong Radio

A woman sings intersection
after intersection
in the gathering dusk.
Listeners can join in—
reciting, in rhythm,
anything over and over;
"One, two, three, four,
five, six, seven..."
Repeat as needed,
as the whole clan
gathers on the trail:
"Grandfather, look at all
these other people
visiting the village!"

Seven Words of Poetry

I.

All this happened on the same day, as I remember— the seven words of poetry, better than anything I could ever write. Spring, 1959, and I had been across town, at college, studying poetry. After school, though, I came bopping, literally, over to the West Side, to work at the store. Parked over there on E Steet, by the big Buddhist temple, and made my way, swinging and swaying, to the very heart of the West Side, 919 F Street, the store.

It's not there anymore, neither is most of the West Side business district; it's been obliterated, "war-torn," by Urban Renewal, but in those days we had four movie theaters to choose from, and all the food we could muster. And oh, the continual and pervasive music—jazz, blues, mariachis—streaming over the streets from bars, shine parlors, restaurants, pool halls, barbers shops, stores . . . The place was hopping, and you were bopping.

My uncles are on break, making deliveries, whatever; my grandmother, Yoshiko Saito, is taking an order, in Japanese, over the phone. My grandfather, Busuke Saito, is out back, in the sunlight, by an orange tree he planted, placing pieces of salmon to soak in a miso cask.

Who is he? What is he like? Well, let's just say that he's ready. He's always been *ready,* and he's *readier* than you are. He's old, fast, muscled, smart. You don't mess with him—unless you want to be chased down the street with a knife. This is him, this is the guy— who came over here in 1907, and never looked back. Started, invented, designed, founded this store from scratch, he did; raised five kids, including a dentist, a pharmacist, a teacher; and when he went to camp, he took his store and home with him— that is, he entrusted them for whatever duration to long-standing and trusted friends, an Italian family. And when he got back, he hit the ground running.

This is the guy who, until 1952, was considered an "alien"—a taxpaying "alien" not permitted to own land in his own name; this is the guy who, when allowed to become "naturalized," was the first in line at the courthouse to become a bona fide American. Passed the exam, in English, with flying colors, and then, flying those colors, went riding the Greyhound to see *his* country—Grand Canyon, Niagara Falls, New York City, Washington, D.C. (And all the souvenirs he brought me said "Made in Japan.")

This is also the guy who was proud of his English, and who was proud of my schooling; thus, every year, he gave me a new pen. The old man, then, was the first one to whom I made this announcement: "Grandpa, guess what? I just got a scholarship. I'm going to Iowa to become a writer."

(I'm not so sure any of my grandparents ever set foot on a college campus. So he thought about what I said, for a minute, while handling the salmon.)

Then: "Good. That's good, Rho-sohn. You go Iowa. You be writer."

Pause. Salmon. Miso. Sunlight. Then: "You know, I just think. When I first come this country, I only know four word English. But those four word, they good for anywhere you go America. Yah. You go anywhere America, those four word good."

"Well, gee, Grandpa— what are those four words of English?"

Pause. Salmon. Miso. Sunlight. Then: *"Cup coffee, piece pie."*

II.

My grandmother was packaging tofu and fish for an elderly woman, a lifelong friend. We exchanged greetings, and when the woman left, I revealed my news to Grandma, who smiled and immediately said, in Japanese: "Oh, so you'll be out there by Des Moines!" What kind of woman is this? The best— warm, funny, sharp, and we had many a laugh out of what happened next.

This middle-aged guy comes in, see, in a suit— maybe a lost tourist, an out-of-place professor, maybe some kind of inspector, because he just stands there, inspecting. He stares, wide-eyed, in wonderment, at all the ordinary stuff: bright fishcakes, gleaming tofu, colorful canned goods from Japan, various announcements in calligraphy, all the whole fish from all over on ice, live crabs, live clams, live abalone, piles of octopus and squid, and then he sees, of all things, a live grandmother.

Who can handle all this. So she goes up to him, ready to make a sale, use the scale, scale, gut, slice, wrap, whatever, when he says: "My, oh, my! This is quite some place you've got here! Why, it's like being in a museum! Tell me, mama-san—how long have you been in this country?"

"Come today fresh!"

Memory

Memory is an old Mexican woman
sweeping her yard with a broom.
She has grown even smaller now,
residing at that vanishing point
decades after one dies,
but at some times, given
the right conditions—
an ordinary dream, or practically
anything in particular—
she absolutely looms,
assuming the stature
she had in the neighborhood.

This was the Great Valley,
and we had swept in
to do the grooming.
We were on the move, tending
what was essentially
someone else's garden.
Memory's yard was all that
in miniature, in microcosm:
rivers for irrigation,
certain plants, certain trees
ascertained by season.
Without formal acknowledgment,
she was most certainly
the head of a community, American.

Memory had been there forever.
We settled in around her;
we brought the electricity
of blues and baptized gospel,
ancient adaptations of icons,
spices, teas, fireworks, trestles,
newly acquired techniques

of conflict and healing, common
concepts of collective survival . . .

Memory was there all the while.
Her house, her shed, her skin,
were all the same— weathered—
and she didn't do anything, especially,
except hum as she moved;
Memory, in essence, was unmemorable.

Yet, ask any of us who have long since left,
who have all but forgotten that adulterated place
paved over and parceled out by the powers that be,
and what we remember, without even choosing to,
is an old woman humming, sweeping, smoothing her yard: Memory.

SECTION III

Jazz

Jazz

I.

The music speaks for itself. And it certainly spoke to me. It *called* me, *called* me by my name: "Laaawwwson! Laaawwwson!" And I certainly listened. Yes, I listened to its warm and gentle voice, its soothing, beautiful voice as it told me, told me, showed me its home, that special place.

And I was there again. Next to the fish store, at the Home of The Music. And where it lived was big and bright and red and yellow and shiny. How could I forget? Bon Ton Jenny's Bar, visiting The Music. The Music knew me. Everybody knew me. And they would laugh and clap as I would dance and sing—with The Music.

And when Grandma came to get me, I would dance and sing on the sidewalk in the broad daylight—with The Music. I would dance and sing in the fish store, and when I got home, I would dance and sing some more—with The Music.

And then The Music disappeared. But here it was again—calling me, talking to me, showing me, soothing me. The Music, yes—I could feel it again.

"Hey, Lawson—what're you doing?" "Nothing. Just listening." "So come on in. It's cold outside." And there, wonder of wonders, was not just a radio, but a *record player*. And the man said: "You like that?" "Yes." "You wanna hear it again?" "Yes." "You know what it is?" "Yes—'Mood Indigo' by Duke Ellington." So I just stood there, and listened.

And when I went outside again, it was certainly "mood indigo"—winter dusk, Jerome Camp, Arkansas. But The Music was there, for our reunion.

II.

My father is deaf in one ear, so he was 4-F during the war. Nevertheless, he was "enlisted" by the government for work in a munitions factory in Chicago. So he and some other men went there from Amache Camp—"stationed" on the South Side. When he came back, he gave me, bestowed upon me, some gifts: records by Fats Waller and Fatha Hines. Fats, he said, had recently died—but he had seen Fatha. And he also told me about a blind pianist named Art Tatum.

Now, of course, I couldn't listen to the records—but I could *see* the music. And I could read the labels, and I could *see* Chicago. It was really something, see—my father and friends looking like "Mexicans" among all the "Negroes," who had all these places, like Bon Ton Jenny's, full of jukeboxes and musicians and dancing. Can you imagine that?

And I mean to tell you—guys like Fats and Fatha and Art could really play some piano! You should hear 'em. Yes, indeed, kid—those guys are really doing something in the great big world out there!

Later on, my dad and I walked over to the shower house. Towels around our necks. Sand at our feet. Dusk, in the desert. People greeted him, welcomed him back; they called him "Doctor," and he was highly respected—even when he drove the butcher truck, he was still "Doctor." Coming back, warm and clean, glowing, all the stars were out. We paused; he was teaching me how to whistle. So I whistled, and then we whistled, "Melancholy Baby," his song, loud and clear—and glowing on the horizon, I could *see*, I could *hear*, Chicago.

III.

Let's pause a bit on this poetic plateau, to see what happens. The camp is dismantled; the people are released to make their way across deserts and mountains, to wherever they consider home. The boy, his dad, the family, return to Fresno.

The records, those fragile items, are packed, carried and finally played. They become the cornerstone of a collection, which continues to this day. The grooves of those records provide a path, a way, a vision, a direction— which continues to this day. The music is tradition, legacy.

Those records are never broken. The music is an enduring philosophy—of adaptability, ingenuity, creation; of humor, wisdom, resourcefulness; of individuality and collectivity; of power and empowerment; of the strength and beauty of the human spirit.

Moreover, it is a *functional* music, for both body and soul, functioning equally well in secular situations and places of worship. The music is a testament to life, to love of life. The music is America's gift to the world. And the practitioners of the music are, undeniably, among the *greatest artists the world has ever known.*

IV.

Ah, to be so "culturally-deprived"! The poor West Side—we had no library, no galleries, no museums, no civic orchestra, no ballet company! To be so impoverished, to eke by on the basic "ABC's" of life—Asian, Black, Chicano cultures, whatever they had to offer: folk festivals of primitive origin, amateur art on available walls, whatever foods could be mustered.

Still, despite the deprivation, we managed to exist with a modicum of grace and style. And, being an illiterate lot, we squandered our money on entertainment, on music, mostly—putting nickels in pervasive jukeboxes, saving wages for when the wandering minstrels came to town, from Mexico, from Texas, from the Deep South and beyond. The posters went up, and in came the "revues."

Moreover, the music we most loved and played and used was Negro music. It was something we could share in common, like a "lingua franca" in our "colored" community. And in our distorted reality of aliens and alienation, it even felt like *citizenship*. It seemed so very *American*—"un-foreign," on "un-foreign" instruments—and the words it used were *English*. Not "across town" or "Hit Parade" English, perhaps, but nevertheless an English that, in its own way, did the job. (And we were all criticized, continually corrected and ridiculed in school for the way we talked—for having accents, dialects, for misusing, abusing the language.)

But the music spoke to us, and we spoke back—laughing and carrying on among ourselves in a quaint code of "jive" and "hepcat" talk about "boogie" and "bebop" and being "cool." Mexicans, Negroes, Orientals —talking that talk! It did the job, and those same kids would even play that music, on school instruments, at talent assemblies in school. The teachers must have figured: "Oh, why not? If that's what they want to do." (As long as they don't abuse the instruments.)

We were quaint, ignorant, primitive, and deprived. We only knew what we knew, had what we had. It was our community's fault. It was the fault of the jukeboxes, which were our libraries; it was the fault of the Chinese-owned record stores; it was the fault of all those touring minstrel "revues" that kept us where we were—incorrigible, unimproved.

We didn't know anything. And all we knew—in detention, on suspension, in special education, on probation—were obscure irrelevancies, certain "tunes" by a Big Joe Turner, by a T-Bone Walker, by a Sister Rosetta Tharpe, by a Hamp, by a Bullmoose, a Cleanhead, a Bird, a Dizzy, a Pres. And, yes, we also knew The Globes—a touring minstrel troupe, a "jazz revue" in shorts employing irrelevant stratagems, bopping about to the tune of "Sweet Georgia Brown."

So by the time we were seniors in high school, we were totally unprepared to deal with the greater world. For example, we didn't learn a thing in Mr. Bramblett's senior civics class. It just didn't take. And about the only thing I remember was that fine spring morning over by the windows, sitting and chatting before class with Sam Jones, Theo Grice, Maureen Dong, and Harumi Okamura, when Yvonne Harvey came in and whispered: "Bird is dead." That was our civics lesson for the day.

And when we graduated, we did what we could do—a group of us made our way to a concert in San Francisco, featuring Sarah Vaughan and Oscar Peterson. I was with my parents, because this was my graduation gift from them; thus, the next night, they snuck me in (I had just turned seventeen) to The Blackhawk Club to hear Dinah Washington, and the next night we saw none other than Earl "Fatha" Hines! The music, yes—a gift that lasts.

v.

About a year later, there's an 18-year-old kid—ostensibly a student in the area—hanging around The Blackhawk Club again. He's still underage, but the waitresses don't know that; besides, he seems to be a "friend" of the musicians, or at least they acknowledge him when he says "Hi, Miles" or "Hello, Coltrane." They say things like, "Hey, man," and "What's happening?"

On this night, however, he's gone outside during intermission. It's cold, foggy, and he's leaning against the wall under a streetlight. No one else is around. Except for another person, a woman—likewise leaning against the wall. It's quiet. A car goes by, tires hissing in the mist. The young man, the woman, stare into space.

After a while, in a hushed voice, he speaks: "Excuse me—but may I have your autograph?" Her face lights up as she smiles: "Why certainly, son! What's your name?" He tells her, and she pronounces it, somewhat "sings" it, as she writes in the book. Then, still smiling, she looks him straight in the eye and says: "You were here last night." "Yes, I was, ma'am. I've been here all week."

And you might say he never left. And what she wrote in that book, her book, was this:

For Lawson
Sincerely
Billie Holiday

And before he knew it, he was writing poetry.

In/Vocation

for Mal Waldron

From the being of me, this
receptacle I am,
I seek and reach
this particular pattern of clouds
clustered on the close horizon,
the ascension of sunlight on the mountains
and the procession therein,

become then, in the sequence,
the presiding precedence of things,
the ordered immediacies,
this graceful grove of trees
meditating
essence of forest
and the slow wind that stirs the sinews,
stimulating the accumulation

of small birds at their calling,
foraging for what abides with winter,
the stuff of what renews
me among grasses and leaves,
the ridges and hollows

of the whole,
entire congregation of collective memory—

choruses, patterns in accordance
with density, intensity,
with destiny—

these sing, these glory, these bring
me pleasure and it spreads through the air
to where you are now,

likewise gifted with gratitude
gracing the brilliant
corners of enclaves
praising rain, this abiding rain
that brings us, takes us, keeps us
huddled in harmonies
now, as deserts, tundras, cities
signal dawn:

Charging, Recharging:
Chanting, Enchanting:

Arise, Arise, Arise, Arise, Arise!

Two Variations On A Theme By Thelonious Monk As Inspired By Mal Waldron

INTRODUCTION: MONK'S PROSODY

> "I can't do that right. I have to practice that."
> —Thelonious Monk, composer, to his pianist
> (himself) during a solo run-through of
> "Round Midnight," April 5, 1957.

April 5, 1957: Maybe I'm sitting on a fire escape in Berkeley, trying to write some poetry. I know one thing: I was listening to Monk by then—particularly his solo on "Bags' Groove," on the Miles Davis 10-inch lp. You might say I was studying Monk's prosody—how each time he'd come out of the speakers in a different, distinctive way, and always swinging.

Years pass. Decades. Prosody.

January 15, 1987: I work a duo concert with Mal Waldron. Mal, even while checking out the tuning, makes reference, says hello, to Monk. The next time we blow, I want to do "Blue Monk."

June, 1987: Whenever the next time is, I'll be ready. I work out a linear, horn-like statement; it fits, like an overlay. Then I jump right into the tune and the piano, and blow something from the inside out—percussive—particularly building around and repeating "ricochet."

April, 1988: One of those long Oregon dusks. Larry Smith, editor of *Caliban*, calls up to ask if I'd be interested in doing something with Monk's prosody. Prosody—yeah. I have to practice that.

I. "Blue Monk" (Linear)

Solid, as the man himself would say.
Solid, as the man at his instrument.
Solid, as the solid composition.

However, at the same time,
this elegant melody,
"Blue Monk,"

while certainly being solid enough—
as evidenced by
the ease of our ability
to hum and whistle it,
even in sleep—

is actually solid, fluid,
and a real gas combined;

you know what I mean:
like feelings, like atmosphere,
like right, like here,

you feel like you've been hearing
"Blue Monk" forever,
since the planet started dancing,
like it's been around since sound,

since the blue wind got up
one blue summer morning,
looked across the cool, blue canyon
at that sweet, blue mountain,
and melodiously started to sing
"Blue Monk";
 you know that lovely feeling,
"Blue Monk";
you know what

"Blue Monk" can do for you,
the melodious message it sends,
the melodious message that always comes
echoing back across the canyons as a result;
"Blue Monk,"

as a result of recognition,
as a consequence of confirmation,
as an accomplishment of affirmation—
"Blue Monk,"
"Blue Monk"
in the sun and rain, in all conditions;

and the song, therefore,
just by being what it is—
these huge, blue feelings
spaced and placed just so,
ascending,
these huge, blue feelings
descending, just so,
and including some delightful
dimensions for refreshment
on a huge, blue plateau—

"Blue Monk," then, by it very nature,
built into its basic structure,
encompasses and contains
all the properties of nature:

take a hold of it,
hold it up to the light;
see what I mean?—
"Blue Monk" has you dancing;

by now you're feeling confident about the song,
feeling like you've got it down,
feeling like you're part of its beauty,
feeling like it's part of you—
which is certainly true;

feeling fine with the freedom of it;
feeling like going for it
with expansiveness, abandon;

feeling exhilarated in your bones
like you want to do something about
exercising your own right
to rhythm and expression;

yes, you feel like you own the song—
which you certainly do—
since you went right down there on West 52nd Street
and got it directly from the man himself,
Blue Monk, who turns out to be,
not the imposing artist you had heard and read about,
but just the husband, the father, the neighbor
making his way out of the corner grocery
with some snow peas and stalks of celery
sticking out of a paper sack;
he just needs something back,
gladly giving you the tune
in exchange for a proven recipe of your own;

meanwhile, Blue Monk is smiling
that solid Blue Monk smile
while offering you directions for usage:

   "Look, 'Blue Monk' is a solid song;
   you can bend it; you can break it;
   you can always remake it;
   it's hot and it's cool,
   it's suitable for digging

in whatever occasion you choose—
ceremonious, thelonious and such . . ."

Ah, the sheer joy of such ownership!
You take "Blue Monk" home and set it
glowing in your living room
like a luxurious lamp.
You stick it in the phone,
sending it out via satellite:

"Hello, Mom? Dig this song!"
"Hello, is this the White House?
Listen, I've got a solid
new anthem for the shaky republic!"

You take "Blue Monk" outside to the fire escape,
seeing how far you can throw it,
looping it smoothly over the moonlit harbor
as it becomes a bridge
of flowing blue lights:
"Blue Monk."
You're dancing, humming,
strolling slowly across,
tossing blue notes
floating over the wide, blue water
like you're a luminous, musical spider;
tossing cool, blue clusters high overhead,
creating a blue, musical constellation:
"Blue Monk";

by now, many others,
including birds, animals, insects,
have joined you on your excursion,
having just got wise
to mythology and fireworks combined,
staring awestruck up into the huge, blue night
to find the Blue Monk profile outlined,
pointing out and humming

each huge, blue star in the melody—
and, oh, those sweet, blue spaces in between . . .

Yes, indeed, this is some kind
of luxurious structure,
an architectural legacy

ascending, descending, with pliable plateaus
for ease of breathing, handling,
relaxing, building, dancing, laughing,
praying, creating, embracing, enhancing;

a structure as solid, fluid, strong,
translucent, luminous, freeing,
and bracing
as the man himself—

Mr. Blue Monk,
bringing everything we do,
we see, we know,
into melodious focus

through the blue keys
of his blue piano;

therefore, in this blue region,
with this blue vision, in this blue
body of being
we all know as home,
everything throbs and pulses and glows
with the true, blue beauty of his song:

   "Blue Monk"!

II "Blue Monk" (percussive)

Ricochet:

Radius:
Radiating:

Reciting: Realizing: Referring: Recapturing: Repercussion:
Revolving: Reflecting: Returning: Reconstituting: Republic:
Reshaping: Restructuring: Reversing: Reclaiming: Religion:
Respecting: Removing: Reforming: Receiving: Reality:
Refining: Reducing: Refreshing: Regenerating: Resource:
Regarding: Relating: Relaxing: Revering: Remembering:
Renewing: Revising: Repairing: Replacing: Residing:
Reviewing: Respecting: Resolving: Reviving: Responsible:
Retaining: Resuming: Revealing: Rehearsing: Resulting:
Restoring: Retrieving: Regaining: Recovering: Relying:
Redeeming: Replying: Reminding: Rewarding: Resounding:

Reverberating:

Remarkably:

Releasing:

Remaining:

Repeating:

Listening Images

LESTER YOUNG

Yes, clouds do have
The smoothest sound.

BILLIE HOLIDAY

Hold a microphone
Close to the moon.

CHARLIE PARKER

Rapids to baptism
In one blue river.

COLEMAN HAWKINS

A hawk for certain,
But as big as a man.

BEN WEBSTER

Such fragile moss
In a massive tree.

LOUIS ARMSTRONG

Just dip your ears
And taste the sauce.

ROY ELDRIDGE

Get in the car.
Start the engine.

DIZZY GILLESPIE

Gusts of gusto
Sweep the desert.

MILES DAVIS

3 valves, tubing...
How many feelings?

CLIFFORD BROWN

A fine congregation
This spring morning.

ART TATUM

Innumerable dew,
A splendid web.

BUD POWELL

The eye, and then
The hurricane.

70

THELONIOUS MONK

Always old, always new,
Always déjà vu.

COUNT BASIE

Acorns on the roof—
Syncopated oakestra.

DUKE ELLINGTON

Stars, stripes, united
States of Ellington.

GENE AMMONS
CHU BERRY
DON BYAS
EDDIE DAVIS
HERSCHEL EVANS
PAUL GONSALVES
DEXTER GORDON
WARDELL GRAY
RAHSAAN KIRK
HANK MOBLEY
CHARLIE ROUSE
SONNY STITT

Mountain mist,
Monumental totem.

JOHN COLTRANE

Sunrise golden
At the throat.

ERIC DOLPHY

Coming across quick
Deer in the forest.

DELTA BLUES

They broke bottles
Just to get the neck.

SON HOUSE

A lone man plucking
Bolts of lightning.

KANSAS CITY SHOUTERS

Your baby leaves you on the train.
You stand and bring it back again.

BIG JOE TURNER

Big as laughter, big as rain,
Big as the big public domain.

Louis Armstrong

Pops' place is one great kitchen:
the presence of food is dominant,
the cooking constant,
and the source of sauces goes back
who knows how many years—
handed down by the mouthful
to continue the household:
the pride and pleasure
of resourcefulness, regeneration . . .

Thus, Pops is always talking
about licks, and chops,
about putting the pot on,
about his "flavorite" songs, tastiest tunes,
about strutting with some barbecue—
always looking to play that breakfast dance
and then, on Monday, here comes
red beans and rice!
("Appetite is a right,
so don't be wrong!")

In Pops' place, the savor is always strong.
This is how the chicory coffee
steeps and brews,
the seasonings season, to belong.
("If you ain't sweaty,
the sauce ain't ready!")

So even and especially
when he's stewing in the blues,
the exuberance boils over,
exulting in the ingredients of life:
the elements of power and perspective
emanating from the very foundation
where the first hamhock was laid—

the cornerstone course and chorus—
and by noon the roof was made:
"Time for a fish fry and some cobbler!"
Expansive laughter through the rafters . . .

Everybody calls him Pops, except his mother.
She calls him Louis; he calls her Mother.
And between the two of them, the rest of us
are a celebrated musical family.
For what is an orchestra
if not a converted kitchen?

With pots and pans and lids
we have our timpani, percussion.
With brooms we whisk, we baste the rhythm;
with spoons, we tippy-tap tinkle;
ladles dip deep into the bass
of kettles, secure with syncopation.
Bottlecaps and cans—tambourines!
Every tub, every tine, keeping time!

And, oh, all manner of things to blow!
Jugs, bottles, bones,
reeds right out of the salad!
Held just so to the mouth,
all utensils are instruments—
for calling, for answering . . .

Pops' own trumpet is part spatula, part funnel.
He keeps it by the oven, always warm.
Mother flips and stirs things with it.

Anyone can dip it for a sip.
Anyone can blow on it, through it.
It's usually too hot to handle.

Pops grabs it with a handkerchief, for insulation.
He licks it to a festive flavor,

74

for spirit and the gusto,
and when he starts to blow,
you know just how
hungry you've always been
for this food,
this music,
for your very survival—

for what Pops is actually doing
with his singing, his playing,
is offering sustenance
to anyone beyond the porch,
the yard, the widening bayou—
all of it glowing
with the aroma of his sound:

> Pops is calling and calling you!
> Pops is proclaiming the table set!
> Pops is saying don't be late!

> *yes, all roads*
> *parade to Pops' place*

> *for you to follow on home!*

Lester Young

As befitting the President, Lester's residence
is the essence of elegance,
of eloquence and grace.
History, after all, is shaped here,
and strategic negotiations
have monumental consequence.

Pres assumes responsibility, precedence.
There's Pres, and the rest of us.

Not that you'd know it from him.
On the contrary, he exudes
the strength and confidence
of utmost humility—
for Pres is the most gentle of men
(he calls this his "crib,"
as he calls everyone "baby")—
and when our eyes adjust
to the mildest of lights,
the surroundings surprise us
with the intensity
of softness and simplicity—

in keeping with his policy
of public accessibility.

Thus, nothing is taken for granted;
even the commonest subjects
are subject to accountability,
for as the master statesman
states it with his rhetoric:
    "That little slur over there, for instance,
    framed and shaded by a phrase
    just so
    trailing past the trellis

and out into the garden
glowing with Grandmother
at her harvest, captivated
with the fragrance of red roses
as you, a child again, gingerly
hold a handful of her finest flowers
for displaying later in that special
sunlight burnishing her treasured
hand-hewn, hand-me-down table,
her fabled blue-veined vase . . ."

Curiously, or fittingly, in this case,
there are no calendars, no clocks.
Pres holds time in his heart.
Therefore, he is never in a hurry.

So even though he may say,
"I Didn't Know What Time It Was,"
the rest of us better be ready
to *leap* to his lyrical direction,
for when Pres begins a beat
he means it—his subtlest of feet
leading us smoothly through
structures of entrusted legacies . . .

And there is no time
we are more aware of time—
its contours, its hollows,
its incredible fullness
of being who we are with Pres—

  For it is we
  Who are duly elected
  To occupy this elevated,
  Privileged position
  In this federated
  State

Of grace and freedom

Founded for the people

By

The president of love:

Lester Young!

Billie Holiday

Wouldn't you know it?—The Lady has her name
right out front there on the mailbox:

all big and bold, in multicolored lettering.
Except what it says is "Eleanora Fagan."

What kind of place is this for The Lady?
Lady Day, as titled by the Chief Executive—

her with all that class and fame, gardenias . . .

Sure don't look like much to me, no sirree.
Would have passed it by if I didn't know better.

It's what is known as a nondescript setting:
a preplanned subdivision, tract home at that.

Listen to her sing—so you can understand.
Listening to The Lady, you want to turn back.

The act of listening is an invasion of privacy.

You can stand it, though—just don't get close.
You're in the street; she's at the kitchen window.

She's doing what she pretty well please—
cooking, singing, in any getup, so beautiful . . .

And, oh, does she have some mouths to feed!
Papa's home, hungry, and here come Pres and Ben!

You know if you knocked, she'd invite you in.
Make a fuss over you as you fussed with the kids.

Come on in and help me get this stew together!
Get vegetables from the garden! Go follow Mama!

All this chopping to do—don't eat too fast!
Put some mellow music on—let's make it last!

And the music you choose is with her and Pres.
All the love you have comes pouring out again.

Whoever you are, you will never be the same.
This is The Lady's home, the home

     she never had.

Charlie Parker

Yardbird. Bird. Yard.
Whatever he was called, whenever he played,
wherever he heard him, wherever we are now,
Yardbird never left home.

On this corner, of 12th Street and Vine,
Pres and the Basie have just finished a set,
and Big Joe Turner is tending bar and song
with the accomplished embellishments
of Mr. Pete Johnson.

This is Bird's place, and we hear it all.
Why leave this kind of yard?

People are downhome here, and in the know.
Sure, times may be tough,
but that don't excuse the music.
We're serious about it.
Go ahead, Bird, and blow!
If we can't follow you, we ain't worth it.

So there goes Bird deep down in the gutter,
passing the bottle around, taking it back.
So there goes Bird back into the alley
talking that trash, trashing the sack.

Go ahead, Bird! We can dance to it.
If we can't dance, we can't use it.
We've cut off the sides of our shoes for you.

So there goes Bird all around the corner.
Mr. Preacherman Bird, going into a storefront
and coming out with a sanctified sermon.
Now here comes the whole congregation—
looking happy, feeling fancy, dancing!

Go ahead, Bird, Yardbird, Charlie!
Whomever he are, comes transportation:

come a taxi, come 52nd Street,
come Harlem, come New York City,
come Bud rubbing a glass piano,
come Monk meandering in the dark,
come Dizzy blowing the roof off,
come Klookamop, come Max making wax,
come Miles and miles of open sky,

come bebop and everybody else,
come the enhancement of anybody's life.

Come Yardbird right into your home.
Come Charlie beside you at the station.
Come Bird sneaking up with the blues.
Come Yard surprising from inside of you.

If you have blood, and pulse,
if you have heart—then there you are.
Welcome to the corner. You never left home.

Bud Powell

"Parisian Thoroughfare"

Shops gleaming wares,
windows streaming with the streets of commerce as fragrance
from a nearby bakery fills and gilds the air
burgeoned to the brim with birds, butterflies, blossoms,
rising and falling
calls of children quickening the courtyards,
women whisking walks in the sunlit
briskness of rhythm
propelling, pulsing the entire populace, the entire
thoroughfare into action after the night's refreshing rain
promising spring thick with brilliance,
the surprising
turn of events where everything turns out happy . . .

("Hey, cut it, man!")

John Coltrane

Coltrane's home is the oldest home there is.
It is older than houses; it is older that clothes.
It is older than shelter; it is older than us.

It says so in the scripture of the structure.

There was light; there were the elements.
There came a clearing in the forest.
There came, then, the great encampment.

Oh, there were places to stay, then,
to get out of the wind and the rain.
As we moved on, we took the sky with us.

Then came some lean-to, some little cabin.
The rest is history; the music, testament.

Who knows what else this place has been?
As we moved on, the moon came with us.

Domicile, shrine, mortuary, mosque . . .
Whatever we conducted there was business.
And what it was, was always simultaneous:

a humble cottage, a healer's secular office,
main headquarters of the underground surface . . .

> *Is that a train I hear?*
> *A call to prayer?*
> *Who walks the constellations?*
> *What river is near?*

Whatever this is, it is a house of worship.
This is the temple of the soul and spirit.
This is the temple of all gods, manifest.
This is the temple of the sun and stars.
This is the temple of the abiding reverence.

There. There. There, now. There. There.

84

Re/Collections

"When I play my music I am not play-
ing about anything else at all. I'm not
putting down anything that you could
express in words. I don't play about
Religion or the universe or love, or
hate, or soul. All of that might be
there but not any specific one. You
can take from it only what you bring
to it. I don't play words."
      —Marion Brown, "Recollections"

When I play my music
I may be
standing in a field
after rain,
singing my praises
to the sun.

When I play my music
I may be
making my way
across a windswept beach,
a sea conch at my lips,
letting it speak for me.

When I play my music
I may be
humming through
the lower register
of a mysterious city—
when I play my music,
when I play my music.

When I play my music
I may be
resonating with a reed

at the wide river's edge,
calling and calling
what comes to me,
what comes to me
when I play my music.

When I play my music
I may be
whistling with the wind
accompanying me,
propped on a precipice
overseeing my flock
at dusk
in the desert—
when I play my music,
when I play my music.

When I play my music
I may be
blowing through
the sweet bamboo
of a rainswept forest,
responding to the sounds—
drop by drop by drop—
letting my presence
be known.

When I play my music
I may be ministering
to a congregation
raising our voices
in ceremony,
in celebration.

When I play my music.
When I play my music.

When I play my music

I may be
hungry;
I may be
angry;

I may be
grieving;
I may be
leaving;

I may be
praying;
I may be
staying;

when I play my music,
when I play my music.

When I play my music
I am
surrounded by sound,
the tone of being,
reverberating, breathing.

When I play my music
I am
sound;
I am sound;
I am being.

When I play my music.
When I play my music.

Come to me, then.
Come to me, then.
Come to me, then,
with your
melodious messages,

with your
harmonious heritages.

Come to me, then,
with your
burdens,
with your blessing.
Come, let us be
music together.

Move, as the spirit
moves.
Move, as the earth
moves—
turning and turning
in tune
with the spirits,
with the stars.

Yes, there is
enough for us—
here, here.

Take from me.
Bring to me.
In this music.
In this music.

We are.

The Theme

for Johnny "Hammond" Smith

The theme is free.
The theme is free.
The theme is free.
The theme is free.

Thank you thank you thank you thank you thank you,
as the performance draws to a close,
as the stage transforms itself
into ordinary space,
as the music is dismantled,
as people become people—

audience, poet, musician
making their way into the regular world of usual illusion

that in itself is a theme.
The thematic ramifications of, say,
traffic and sprinklers,
the passage of musical time
through poetic parking lots,
the symbolic manifestation
of blue shoes, green trees, prospects of purple

horizons proclaiming what is.

Likewise, we're free and for the taking.
Thematically embellished,
dramatically gifted,
and guaranteed to last a lifetime—
distinctive, congruent,
and made to stay that way.

What takes, keeps. Gives
semblance in the coexistent hours—
waking, sleeping—
those in-between places
when the mood comes over you like those voluminous, proverbial
clouds storming
desperation or not at all because you've had it
up to here with what deems itself to be
relative to related tragedy in showers
as a consequence of inundation
by neon bleeding from confiscated
canisters parading tubes of boulevards—

and where are *you* again?

You know you're in the garden.
Why say you're in the graveyard?
So wait a blessed second, my illustrious friends.
You know what it takes to be
thematically
sound in the ground,

you know what it takes to seed soil,
work the sweet earth blissful with the wet wit of given elements

to whistle
these fragrant statements,
humming for harvest
through the ceremonial
membranes of collective memory

which provide, then, you know, lyrical
avenues of evanescence, pathways to,
you know, what stand to be corrected
by the balance,
you know,
of power
of melody,

the sheer, you know,
force of harmony
of being here and feeling
fantastic about it—

tapping your feet,
tapping your mind,
tapping your root
with your own free, fine and happy
will to do, you know, something cool, sweet and snappy about it.
Why not, you know, why not?

So, hey, folks—
you know we're a whole
chorus
of us.
You know we're a major congregation
making a morning raid on life.
I thank you, we thank
one another for these
thematic statements that grace this existence.
We're grateful.
It's beautiful, you know,
it's mutual.

And as for Mr. Johnny "Hammond" Smith,
that remarkable individual,
well, let me move on over,
get out of the way,
and listen to what he has to say:

Oregon

Oregon

I took the long way to get here. As a matter of fact, I didn't even know this was my destination, but destiny has an interesting way of working: the one and only college T-shirt I had as a child was an oversized thing an uncle gave me, and on it was the University of Oregon Duck. Other than that, Oregon was a rumor—some place "north of Sacramento," wherever that was.

So instead of the Oregon Trail, I hit the Poetry Road, the Jazz Path, out of Fresno in 1960. Strapped my mother's old typewriter atop my big string bass, hitched up the horses, and was off—off to seek my fortune. (My fish-store uncles pronounced the instrument as if it was "bass"—and they were right: My "scales" stank as I whaled away "for the halibut." I finally abandoned the fish in New York, setting it free in the ocean.) Ah, the alternate route—of verse and reverse . . .

Got to Kansas City at dawn; strummed a bit for Pres and Bird, then headed in the direction of Iowa—sent, sentenced, by my poetry senti-nel, Phil Levine. (And where, unbeknownst to me, my mail-order bride from Missouri, unbeknownst to her, was awaiting our meeting.) Then, when our covered wagon reached Chicago (!), I turned right into a blizzard. Beat back the Cleveland Indians and got to New York, New England, and stayed a spell. But my tofu was a-gettin' low; my supply of tortillas was running out; we were scraping the bottom of the barrel; so this time, for sure, with a real map, we hit the actual Oregon Trail.

Got to Oregon in 1965, just in time to escape The Sixties. We're ten miles from the California border (sixty miles from the nearest camp, Tule Lake, where 18,000 of us were encamped on Modoc land), and we'd go up on Siskiyou Pass and watch California shake, rattle, and roll. There were flames all over, and we'd have to fend off dusty droves of "drybacks" trying to flee across the border. In the meantime, we had founded, by planting an ash tree in Ashland, the Free Federation of the New Fresno Republic on the greater West Side of Oregon. Anthems, we have (plenty, from my collection), and my wife (a teacher) and sons (a painter and a philosopher) are always dreaming up new ideas, high concepts, for other all-important means of affiliation and identifica-tion, namely, T-shirt, bumper sticker, license plate. The flag is the sky; everyone is welcome.

Appreciating Oregon

To appreciate what Oregon has, and is,
you have to imagine that Oregon doesn't exist.
That is, imagine that you're driving
north from San Francisco to Seattle
and when you reach the "Bay of Oregon"
the interstate makes a long swing to the right.

A very long swing, that is—skirting the shore
of this gigantic body of water
lapping and overlapping the borders
of California, Nevada, Idaho, and Washington . . .

Thus, before you left on such a considerable journey,
you certainly considered your options:

    1. Flying;
    2. Riding the relaxing but expensive
        "I-5 Ferry" for 2 days and nights;
        these great, seagoing vessels
        negotiate the bay in style,
        offering all the comforts of home;

        take your pick of unique cruise ships:
        "The Portland Trailblazer,"
        "The Salem Legislator,"
        "The Eugene Duck,"
        "The Roseburg Bohemian,"
        "The Medford Mall."

But you opted to drive after all.
So here you are, cruising along the shore
of northern California, northern Nevada,
hoping to make it to the port city of Payette, Idaho,
by dawn, by afternoon, by nightfall—
whichever comes first, it doesn't much matter,

because it's just land on one side, water on the other,
and it all blends together and becomes rather boring.

Really, now—the great bay known as "Oregon"
is certainly blue and beautiful enough,
but it is, after all, water, water, water,
and you can't wait to get past Walla Walla
to where the Columbia River makes its delta,
where a high and shiny bridge makes you feel
like it's all downhill from there

to where you have reservations at the Red Lion
in Vancouver, Washington, and a seafood dinner awaits you
at the Inn at the Quay, overlooking the bay
as the great ships arrive, moving like mountains,
looming like cities in the water.

A Night in the Valley

I always like to keep
some sesame seeds
in my pocket.

They stay there
with coins, keys, sand,
whatever gathers.

You'd be surprised
how long they keep.

On nights like these,
I reach in
and pull out
a fingerful.

I like the grit
of things,
the spark
of flavor,
the taste
of memory—
the close, the far.

I eat the stars.

My Father and Myself Facing the Sun

We are both strong, dark, bright men,
though perhaps you might not notice,
finding two figures flat against the landscape
like the shadowed backs of mountains.

Which would not be far from wrong,
for though we both have on Western clothes
and he is seated on a yellow spool
of emptied and forgotten telephone cable
and I recline on a green aluminum lounge,

we are both facing into the August sun
as august as Hiroshima and the autumn.

There are differences, however, if you care
to discover, coming close, respectfully.
You must discover the landscape as you go.

Come. It is in the eyes, the face, the way
we would greet you stumbling as you arrive.
He is much the smooth, grass-brown slopes
reaching knee-high around you as you walk;
I am the cracks of cliffs and gullies,
pieces of secret deep in the back of the eye.

But he is still my father, and I his son.

After a while, there is time to go fishing,
both of us squatting on rocks in the dusk,
leaving peaks and tree line responsible for light.
There is a lake below, which both of us
acknowledge, by facing, forward, like the sun.

Ripples of fish, moon, luminous insects.
Frogs, owls, crickets at their sound.
Deer, raccoon, badger come down to drink.

At the water's edge, the children are fishing,
casting shadows from the enormous shoreline.
Everything functions in the function of summer.

And gradually, and not by chance, the action
stops, the children hush back among rocks
and also watch, with nothing to capture but dusk.

There are four of us, together among others.

And I am not at all certain what all this means,
if they mean anything, but feel with all my being
that I must write this down, if I write anything.

My father, his son, his grandsons, strong, serene.

Night, night, night, before the following morning.

At the Stronghold

for Miles and Lowell

Miles is so sufficient
He makes me
Breakfast with a flick of his wrist—

                 little cakes
                 of oceans and islands.

Lowell is into

                 stirring,

Mostly,
But if I ask him

                 he picks the burrs
                 off the tops of my socks.

Then they demonstrate
The adaptability

        of scissors and cardboard,
        making up games
        that rule about life.

I give them
        many-bladed knives,
Little men in blue diving suits

And remember me.

        There's a cool
                Tlingit wind
        Blowing over
        Water all the way from Japan
        Blurring the surface
        Of my eyes,
             the deeps

Pulling me
                down and in.

        *

Up over Greensprings,
The pass, crash
Of wheeled
                cataracts
Screaming logjams
Into and out of
Switchbacks

With a flick of fins.
Eyes. Brown
Eyes of bottles,
                    squirrels
That never learn.

*

Count your
            self
Lucky
To find a deer
            by Pinehurst. Bless

You.
    She
Is the soul
                        of women among huckleberries

Soft, fine eyes

Before the invasion,
The cry.

*

Lately, in the drought,
I am obsessed

By clouds, their
Forming, knowing

Them only as
Dispersal flowing

Over me
Lately

In the drought.

*

K. Falls ain't
Got nothing
For me.

        Unless I had a need
        For gutters, for

        Official termination,

        My brown eyes
        Welling over at the rim

        Brown spit
        Bottoms of bottles,

        My brown spirit
        Slumped in some stirrups

        At the terminal.

*

Hell, I'm not trying to do
Nothing for nobody
But me,

My own cause,
My destiny

Come round
To me.

I need my own
Sense
Shaped into place

In a strong body with
Whole bones
                    with no

Disease in the marrow,
The smolder of shrapnel.

Not even the need
For legend,
                    something

monumental to build on,
                                        something
Grand, just
My self,
My own scope and destiny,

So when my
Time comes, I can go

                    off and die

                    like a man.

*

Captain Jack,
I come to you

In respect,
Out of a need

For communion.

I will not dance and sing
In your sacred cinders

Where even today
The trail
Is difficult to walk upon.

We, too,
Walked upon this ground,
And though our
Stronghold
Was made for us,
To hold us in,

We, too,
Heard the geese in the wind,
The wind in the tules

And dreamed
In our brown bodies

Of peace and the good land,

Of home.

*

And so I come to you,
Captain.

And if you were to meet me
On the difficult terrain
Of a parking lot

You would extend your hand to mine.

*

There is a mystery
How you survived

This desperate place
Of edges and wind.

The commissioners were many.
They bled in the heat.

There were so few of you.
What did you eat?

There is no mystery.
The lava bed is a place to sleep.
Heat, rain, cracked
Sweet cinders, the red
Tule rope of resistance—

This is how we sing and survive—

The entire
One of us
Gorged with the knowledge

Of paved genocide
Trying to find its way here.

*

Here, in this stronghold
I have hid my heart,

A battlement
Strong at the marrow,
Stored here

For when the time allows,

Fists in the throat,
A volley
Of words and rocks
In strong boxes

Back of the heart
Behind mazed
Trails spiraling

To my music,
Where no one is allowed.

Here, in this stronghold,
I hide
Myself
To myself,

Deaf with my pulse
Running through the walls

Where my life is carved,

Ancient signs
Where the hurts happened,
The loves, the births,

All in calligraphy
That nothing but the blood

Deciphers,
Or cares

To be allowed

To this stronghold

Where I show my heart.

     *

"Question 27: Are you willing to serve in the armed forces of the United States, in combat duty, wherever ordered?"

No.

"Question 28: Will you swear unqualified allegiance to the United States of America and faithfully defend the United States from any and all attack by foreign or domestic forces and foreswear any form of allegiance to the Japanese emperor, or any other foreign government, power, or organization?"

No.

Hirohito?
Him people
like you na me.
Me no go
Chinchinahtee.
Me go
Tule Lake.
Me stay
Carifonia.
Home.

*

All I wanted
Was a place to live,

How we had always known,

Women among huckleberries,
Tules that teach
Children of junipers, geese, and sky.

All I wanted
Was to fight to live,
To be left alone.

All I wanted
Was a concession to dignity,
Our own reservation.

All I wanted
Was our own
Defeat.

All I wanted
Was to die.

*

Looking into the eyes
                of my children,
                the gifted young

Who wished me in women's clothes,
Who silently called me
                white and compromiser,

I see the *why*

    I am

The renegade
I am,
The revolutionary
I will always be.

What land we had
We must have back again.
This is the stronghold,
The heart, the spirit,
The land, the heart.

This termination, this
Extermination, this
Compromise to survive.

The fenced-in barracks
Still stand
Beyond the ancient carvings
Of Prisoner Rock.

The signs are right.
The spirit. The land.
We must have back again.

Those of us still alive
Singing assimilation
With the flick of wrists,
Thrive on the sick
Blood of subjugation
Here on this very land
Where we died.

Captain Jack
Will be hanged
Tomorrow. *"Instruction
To all persons
Of Japanese ancestry . . ."*

This is the stronghold,
The heart, the molten
Flow solidified
Blood of ancestors.

The blood of us
Is the red tule rope.

What are you worth
In the eyes
Of your sons?

The blood of us
Is the red tule rope.

*

As our stay increases—

summer into fall—

The wounds and pain
fall from our feet

As we begin to know
The paths
Of the stronghold
The scars of battle
Smooth places
To stand upon

As our stay
Increases
To the span
Of our life

As we begin to see
Buttes and geese,
Juniper and sky

As all clouds
Form at Shasta
And return there.

Captain Jack,
Father,

You teach us

To stand
To plant
Our feet in the ground

You teach us

To stand
To raise
Our eyes from the ground.

*

My sons,
You are beside me now.

No.
You will not be leaving
For Oklahoma.

No.
No one will take your photo
In front of barracks.

Yes.
We are willing to serve.

Yes.
We swear allegiance.

And if my old time is allowed,

I will go off into the hills

With the flute of my father
And sing the song

    Of geese in the wind

    Of wind among tules

    Of the red tule rope

    Of blood that always flows

    Of clouds around Shasta

    And listen, and grow

    Silent and still

    In my own, in my own

    Wisdom and dignity

    As a man.

From Left to Right

"El Jarabe Loco"
—Dominio Público

The wind usually dies down at night, in the valley.
It comes in from left to right, looking from the kitchen window.
So I always hang the clothes with their back to the wind,
the way I would walk to school in Arkansas, on ice.

A full moon, a full train, from left to right.
And the clothes are out too, so I don't have to do it in the morning.

When the wind will be here, as sure as Mexican music in the night,
which is what get me here, dancing.

I would have it said there was a power and urgency
that could not be denied, no matter what the words read,
despite the education that tried,
the material was always there, faithful, left, and right.

If I had an old quilt, I'd hang it out to dry.
No wind could ever ruffle its images, no sun could fade what it had to say.

You think of art swirling around the head like a self-inflicted halo.
"Art" with quotations, marks not to be trusted.
It has to do with what you say and are than what is imposed upon you,
a halo in the dark that is gone by sunrise, with wind.

I want to be stitchery, with sweat in the seams, to keep
people warm and sweet and strong through the ages.

This song goes from left to right. It hurts to make it.
My throat is tired, quivering, but you can see the images.

A quilt. A train. A line full of clothes.

This and the moon and wind are what I give you.

Good night.

Everything

When the river rose that year, we were beside it
and ourselves with fear; not that it would do anything
to us, mind you—our hopes were much too high for that—
but there was always that remote, unacknowledged possibility
that we had thrown one stone too many, by the handful,
and that by some force of nature, as they called it,
it might rain and rain for days, as it had been,
with nothing to hold it and the structure back,
and with everything to blame, including children
on into late summer and all the years ahead,
when it would be ours to bear, to do much more with
than remember and let it go at that—some mud,
some driftwood, some space of sky as a reminder
before getting on with the world again;
no, the balance was ours to share, and responsibility
for rivers had as much to do with anything
as rain on the roof and sweet fish for supper,
as forests and trembling and berries at sunrise;
thus it was, then, that we kept our watch,
that we kept our wits about us and all the respect
we could muster, sitting in silence,
sleeping in shifts, and when the fire died,
everyone was there to keep it alive;
somehow, though, in the middle of the night,
despite our vigils, our dreams, our admonitions,
our structure, our people, and all our belongings
broke free with a shudder and went drifting away—
past the landing, the swing, the anchored cages,
down through the haunted rapids, never to be found;
when we awoke that morning, the sun was back,
the river had receded under our measuring stick,
and everything had been astonishingly replaced,
including people and pets, the structure intact,
but in the solitude of all our faces as we ate,
the knowledge was there, of what we all had done,
and that everything would never be the same.

Juxtapositions

The shadow of my head
on a flat, black rock
accompanied by,
with the shifting,
shivering branch-tip
of a broad, leafy oak
in an open park
at the corner
of Dawn and Plenty,
a major city;

then, too, a cool
midmorning in Canyonville,
looking into, through,
mist, steam, toppings,
fillings, the many
reflections blending
mountains, lives,
behind, ahead of me,
a bakery window;

Margo, dark
hair and eyes, shining,
turning, breathless
from the dancing,
surprised by light
in this dancing
forest, shining,
turning, breathless,
who died;

tossing a wet
corncob out the window, bits
between my teeth,
wind, the swift

vehicle, crows
on the shoulder,
in the heat,
just to see if it fits;

whenever I see the sign,
I am reminded of many
acquaintances, including
the store owner,
50% off;

making their way through
incredible hardships,
they came, fighting
disease, rapids, inhabitants,
battling the impassable,
with croissants to Oregon;

it was a bird
which caused me to,
by its very nature
of being about
the color and height
of a small deer,
forget, overlooking
the expanse of grass
leading up to
the snowy mountain,
feeding, watching,
crouching, calling
before it flew,
everything I ever knew;

after the pilfering, pursuit,
the fuss, the fume,
you realize that what you've
finally done is put
yourself in a position,

despite yourself, lights
clear down in the valley,
here in the here
of deer, forest, habitat,
and not a minute too soon,
to view the full and rising moon.

Loading Feed in the Grange Parking Lot

Bright sunlight on the Grange parking lot.
A few clouds putting new snow on the mountains.
The asphalt is wet and shiny from the night before.

Two men in heavy jackets are going back and forth
from the storage area to the blue pickup truck.
They are loading sacks of feed. See their breath?

A third man, the truck owner, leans against a fender.
He, too, is breathing mist, as he looks out over
the Cotton Belt and Southern Pacific
freight cars on the tracks, an engine churning
somewhere behind the Grange, over on the left.

But the man doesn't seem to be noticing that.
Instead, his head is tilted upward, over the tracks
and trains, beyond the valley, into the mountains.

Perhaps he is thinking about getting home through snow.
Perhaps he is thinking about unloading his truck—
stacking the feed sacks in his barn, with his son.

Or perhaps he is simply considering
the wonderful, beautiful, arduous cycle of seasons
and how, just yesterday last summer,
when people were harvesting this feed in their fields,
he was just strolling along without a care in the world—

chewing a blade of grass, watching sunlight
shine on the fenceposts, the horses' backs,
and altogether forgetting to remember how
he would be right here at the Grange again, this instant, now.

The Shovel People

It happened by accident: I was in the middle
of my yard in the middle of the morning
in the middle of a hole I was digging
to plant a tree, when all of a sudden,
I heard some cats screaming in the neighborhood—

so, before I knew it, I was dashing down the street
to break up a fight or rescue something
with a shovel in my hand, and

after everything got peaceful, for some reason
or another, there I was, still with my shovel.

Have you ever just stood around with a shovel?
Well, I never had—not when I wasn't digging—
so I decided to take advantage of the situation
and see what would happen, so I started walking.

At first, I carried the shovel in my right hand,
then switched to my left; either way,
the shovel was swinging along as I walked,
in rhythm with me, and once or twice,
I let the handle drag in back,
just for the feel of it, just for the sound.

You might say I was "digging" it, as they say,
because while I looked like a serious man
going to or coming from work, some shoveling job,
I was actually having fun, feeling like a kid
who does things just for the fun of it.

And walking around with a shovel is fun!
For instance, just to feel official,
I switched the shovel to my shoulder
and marched along like I was on some kind of patrol!

Here he comes, there he goes—Mr. Shovelman to the rescue!
Maybe I was a farmer, maybe I was a street worker,
maybe I was a construction worker—all of which I'm not.
But I could be, I thought, if I want. Why not?

Also, since this is a free country,
I walked with my shovel to the corner grocery
to get a candy bar I imagined a shovelman would eat—
something solid but also chewy, with lots of nuts.
And, of course, as a polite person,
I left the shovel outside first, leaning up against
a phone booth for a soft brown dog to watch.

Then I went home—shovel on my shoulder, munching.
I know what you're thinking: "Well, so what?"

Well, I'll tell you: I'm a poet and a teacher
and a son, father, husband. I'm not a weird person.
So I'm not saying that we should all walk around
with shovels on our shoulders and in our hands.
That might look silly, or like we're carrying weapons;
plus, we're not all farmers or workers or soldiers.

But I'll tell you: with that shovel I not only had fun
but felt like I was ready for anything that needed shoveling.
I looked around and noticed what there really was—
mostly things to leave alone, as is, *not* to shovel:
trees and flowers and sand with ants and rocks just sitting
where they were, in empty lots and people's gardens.

Oh, sure, I could have shoveled all those things,
but I had my own tree to plant, my own hole to fill up,
which I did. But I still kept the shovel in my hand.

It began to feel like a friend, so I thought to myself:
"Well, it's a beautiful summer day, and this tool
has helped me dig a hole, take a walk, go on patrol,
think about what I could do if I want, pet a dog,

eat some candy, and just generally appreciate
everything around me that doesn't need shoveling,
and since I planted a tree which gave me
a feeling of accomplishment for a job well done,
and since the tree will grow to give me beauty, shade—
well, I wonder what my friend the shovel would like to do now?"

So the two of us walked up the hill to the middle
of the pasture with the smooth stream running through it.
I washed my hands, I washed the shovel, and in so doing
dipped its full length in the water, then held the handle
as the blade made waves in the water, like a paddle
on a boat called Planet Earth, and I was the Captain.

Then the two of us laid back on the grass and let the sun
dry us, shine us, as birds flew, cows chewed, breezes blew,
and I dreamed about how life would be, could be, with
 The Shovel People.

The Journey South

(TO NORTHERN CALIFORNIA)

I. MOUNT SHASTA

How have you been,
My beautiful friend?

Whenever I see you
Is forever, again.

II. NESS

In a good mood,
I consider adding
ness to everything:
highway-*ness,*
hill-*ness,*
field-*ness,*
sky-*ness,*
river-*ness,*
sun-*ness,*
space-*ness,*
being-*ness.*

III. NOMAD

Looking around the vast landscape,
Alone, leaning on my staff,
I hum a little tune, in Basque.

IV. REST AREA

Sunlight on the asphalt.
Through the wrinkling heat,
Beyond the olive grove—

Pickup trucks gleam
Around an old house.
The sounds of mariachi.

V. STRINGS

Little children,
A big red kite,
A migrant camp.

VI. SACRAMENTO

No wonder
he's smiling—

he's driving
a truckload

of tomatoes!

VII. DOWN UNDER

Bless us,
Eucalyptus.

Thelonious Monk in the Redwoods

Not that he was
ever here,
but I imagine that
sometime, somewhere
in his long career
spanning decades
and generations,

he had to hear
or read the word
redwood
and think about it,
as we all do,
envisioning

just what there is
so evergreen
that stands a while.

And it makes sense,
then, that a man
as visionary
as Thelonious
would allow
that standing vision

to express itself
in a sound composition
(even in some old
New York nightclub),

flowing down
through the trunk
to take true
root on the keyboard—

revealing light
nuances attuned
to bright blue
space and greenery,
redwoods gracing
sunshine and shadow . . .

Not that he was
ever here
as he is,
as you are—now.

Turning It Over

According to Nilak,
it's a custom,
a tradition,
a way of being

to reach
down and turn
over a piece
of driftwood—

"just to
give it some
relief."
See:

```
                                        sun
                      head
                      neck
            arm       arm
         hand      body      hand
            leg       leg

   driftwood    foot      foot
```

ocean ice/shoreline snow/ice/rocks/sand/permafrost tundra/continent

Now, keeping
with that
concept,

consider
this poem
driftwood:

Turn it over!

A Couple of Geese over Phoenix

A couple of geese over Phoenix.
Oregon. And to further
confuse the issue, that species
isn't supposed to be here,
since the unmistakable,
official, national
and international designated
migratory wildlife flyway
is actually across the Cascades
by Klamath Falls, where rising
wave upon wave of wings
come and go in formations
over tules, buttes, and lakes.

It's been that way, unmistakably,
for untold centuries
and so on into history;
thus, to hear descendants
tell of it, these geese
played a part in the seasons
of which there were
many upon many
until the nation intervened.

There's just something about geese,
I guess, that speaks to
qualities of human nature;
thus, waves of geese
flap and call through the verses
of elderly inmates
in the Tule Lake Internment Camp.

I can understand, I guess,

what happened. The conditions
were cloudy with rain
on into the overcast this morning;
you can lose your bearings,
but can gradually
correct your direction
as they did, heading east
over the valley
from the south edge of town.

A couple of geese over Phoenix.
Male, female—obviously a pair,
a couple of geese, mates—
calling, calling, calling...
And even in the parking lot,
it's unmistakable: Fall is in the air.

The Discovery of Tradition

for Toshio Mori and John Okada

I can tell you about this, sure enough,
And I'll do the best job I can
Out here in the perimeters,
But you've got to do it for your self.

And I had been told and told about it,
Studied it, even, square in the face
And gone away wanting from home.
I had to feel it to really know.

What do you do in a case like that?
You don't even know what's missing
And the first thing you've got to do
Is know what it is you need to know . . .

I. THE WORK IN PROGRESS

It was winter (gestures, wind, breathing),
Things needed tending (men in a forest, armloads of wood)
And, of course, I needed tending too (a dropped log rolling
down the slope).

After all, was I to simply
See my self through again,
Repeating what had been done
As its own accomplishment?

What would I see when I looked back,
Emerging into spring and the echoes of children
Calling to me their questions in the lower meadow?

After all, the descent to the valley
Is deceptively easy, and therein lies the task:
To hold your own
Is the most beautiful and natural thing—
But the rest of the world comes
Summoned at the asking,
Implicit in the invitation of your just being here,
And before you know it,
Children have arrived with visitors and leaves with the faces of
Fish and before you know it,
High on the slopes, once more as usual, it starts to snow.

II. THE PROGRESS IN WORK

(Look: a car moving down a road
     banked with snow,
     the tires thick with traction
     grabbing and crunching.)

(Look: a classroom full of flowers,
     sunlight full of books
     and everyone laughing.)

Ah, yes. And still, though,
It had come easy
Because I didn't know any better.

I want to know what I'm doing,
To emerge, to learn, to keep going.

How has it been with you?

III. THE OBSERVANCE OF RITUALS

Toppling, an eclipse off the top of my head now, up there
where the ranges run, the smooth things moving with the wind itself
as it counts, decked out in crevices that matter and laughing
with the whole thing in particular, part and parcel of the what
What are
when the mind is full,

when the life is full,
when there is nothing missing in the eye and senses rocking
back and forth in the continuum
humming with stars, the light winding down and starting up again
to concern us all—
what crosses me crosses you with the force of shadows of sound
emerging and merging into where things quicken and everything
is enough—

rippling, the vision at the bottom of the self, here, down
here as we bob and walk in the moment of momentum and the
Drop off coming
who knows where which is why we keep going into it with the
Force of fortune
we know is there giving back and going forth rippling and toppling

rippling and toppling as we go.

IV. THE EMERGENCE OF TOPICS

It starts to rain. It starts to snow.
Whatever "it" is, it's going through some heavy combinations
Up there in the mountains, mind you,
Whole lot of shaking going on
Including some occasional sunlight, thank you,
And just the whole bunch of stuff in general
And on down the ranks to us in burrows

Tucking heads under wings
The sweet way we like to think
Wet women will always do and did.

I'm sitting here with Toshio and John,
talking over such momentous things:

*"Long ago, children, I lived in a country called Japan. Your grandpa was
already in California earning money for my boat ticket. The village people
rarely went out of Japan and were shocked when they heard I was follow-
ing your grandpa as soon as the money came."*
Toshio Mori,   *Yokohama, California*

*"Two weeks after his twenty-fifth birthday, Ichiro got off a bus at Second
and Main in Seattle. He had been gone four years, two in camp and two
in prison."*
John Okada,   *No-No Boy*

The rain, the snow, the steady stream.
The observance of rituals.
The tribute of tributaries.
The rain, the snow, the steady stream.

This is how it began, for me.

V. THE TRIBUTE OF TRIBUTARIES

The book comes out of the wrist,
With fingers.
It is a pool, an ocean, a delta:

The whorls of words for dreaming in the evening,
The lines of streams to follow on the palm, meandering,
Spaces to see through, to get to and around,
Pages, fingers, forests, frames;

And all of this for holding and waving,
For carrying around.

And this one is Toshio.
And this one is John.

Where had they been before?
Here, here, is the only answer.
Here, as ever more.

Those older ones, those I had always known
Receding into the distance with women,
Holding me at arm's length
Like uncles from mountains,
Gripping steering wheels and going by late
In trucks full of business,
Sometimes handing me
Tickets to a carnival, coins to a show.

Those older ones—
I had to claim them as my own.
I had to sit down with them
In a room ripe with rumor,
Blatant with shadows
And claim them as my own.

And in the end, of course,
It was they who claimed *me,*
Who bade me to be—
Unafraid, unashamed—
Who bade me to see,
Clasping my face
With the faith of love.

"I am your mother's brother."
"I am your father's brother."

"Come."

VI. THE COMING AND THE GOING

We were on the shore that would not be denied.
The ocean filled the eye with wetness of memory
As we were witness to the journey we would know,
The long journey across the *tatami* of water
Away from those who lay sleeping and would go on.

We were on the shore that would not be denied.
It was our own shore, the strength we had known.
We took this with us through the rage and the roar.
We came, we came, to Washington, to California, to Oregon.

VII. THE GOING AND THE COMING

Toshio, being the oldest,
Settled down.
He had had enough of travels and travail,
The hard times cropping up in rows,
And decided instead to learn the language
Of plants and English.

The plants, naturally,
Sprang from his hands
As a matter of course—
They did this all day long;
The English had to be pampered
Under the tip of the tongue
But it, too, came furling from his fingers
Firm and familiar in the rows of his own—
Some nights, they surprised him with dawn.

So he worked hard, and the growing was glorious.
All around were horizons.
What he learned, he earned, and vice versa.
And this allowed John to go to college.

And John was the bright light
come the blackout.
And this allowed us all to go to war.

And it was a strange war of wire
coming at us from all sides.
But Toshio kept writing.

And when the war was over,
John was standing there
In a uniform and a novel.

Sometimes, we would sit watching the world
March by the living room, gesturing and threatening;
But Toshio pointed out the frost on the wisteria
Barbed with beauty in the softness of the light;
And John showed how the eyes of the hysterical
Froze at the lashes, barbed and blurred.

I learned there, the power of the word.

VIII. THE POWER OF THE WORD

And so, in the middle of winter,
In the middle of mountains,
In the middle of night,

In the middle of a room,
In the middle of my hands,
I found my way again.

And so, in the middle of my life,
I found my way to you.

XIX. THE FREEDOM OF TRADITION

Lest it seem too dramatic or mystical, allow me to assure you that of what I speak is in reality very real—that is, it's a *feeling* I'm talking about, which is very natural and how we really live, which is very dramatic and mystical.

And what it's done for me is give me the feeling that I have so much more to give.

Tradition is a place to start.

X. THE RHYTHM OF TRADITION

(water boiling) Well,
(voices outside) it's
(someone launching a boat somewhere) about
(Just the other day, some of us folks
were making mochi in Henry's backyard, using the big
hollowed-out hip and torso of an oak stump for a holder
and an ax handle stuck into half a baseball bat as the pounder)
that (and we, the hands, including Toshio and John,
looked up between the force of our strokes
and smiled, since mochi-making
brings your energy out into the rice and air
where it can be shared again) time
(and Henry, blowing thick mochi breath
into the thick mochi sky, said,
"I wonder if we're the only ones in town doing this now.") again
(And I said, "Maybe in the state, maybe in the nation,
maybe in the entire world because it's night over there and . . ."
And Henry said, "So someone's making love."
And we all began to laugh
because mochi-making is also a continual process) to
(and is going on all the time:) say
(the rhythm of tradition.) good-bye.

In So Doing

I. IN SO DOING

The blue jay
Takes flight
In the pine,

In so doing,
It becomes,
As large
As your life
And mine.

II. CLEARING

There's nothing
Quite like
Clearing
Your throat
In the forest.

III. KEEP QUIET

It won't
Rain tonight.
The stars
Just can't
Keep quiet.

IV. JUST MADE IT

I look at the tree
As if I had
Just made it.
I count the leaves.

V. MIGRANTS

Finally,
The migrants
Arrive
To harvest
My orange
Berries.

VI. PUT THERE

The wind chime
Swings from
A string
Of barbed wire
I put there.

VII. VENTRILOQUISTS

You took
The words
Right out
Of my mouth.

VIII. THE LIST

Where is
The list
Of things
To *not*
Worship?

IX. FOREST FAMILY

Pine cones

Beneath

Pine trees.

X. PLEDGE

Repeat after me:

I

Do

You

We

Be.

(Repeat as necessary.)

Janet

The sunlight of her hair.
The shape of luminous
water filled with leaves.
The song of wind
going to pieces in the pines.

With nothing better
to say, or do,
than look at one
another, and smile,

while planting in the afternoon.

Things As They Are

for Janet

I've looked for things
along this road before—things
of value, things of importance,
and some little things
that just happened to get lost.

Such things happen: things
get blown, forgotten, tossed,
there's wind, accidents,
and any manner of incidents
and creatures to make things
taken, hidden, in the yard,
pasture, along with the ditch
doing drainage and storage.

And the thing is, I don't
even live there anymore.
It's been years. I was not
looking for anything
when I happened to stop,
pull over, and stay put
in the gathering dark.

Things were in process.
We were passing plates,
sharing small talk about
school, people, pets,
and, along with the music,
everything was okay
and pretty much in place.

What happened next? Things
happened to happen and we

were in the middle of it
as walls parted and losses
took effect, scattering
things about in the process

of how we came to find
things as they are: oak trees
smelling of roses, gold-flecked
birds warbling under blue-green
clouds parting to reveal
the newest moon and secret stars . . .

What can I say? It's been years.
We lost, we sought, we found,
and, in the process, some
things still need to be missed

as we gather up our things to carry on,
as we gather up our things to carry on.

SECTION V

Performance

Performance

One of the most gratifying things for me, as an artist, has been the development, the emergence of an *audience*. Various perceptions have changed or disappeared; various barriers have come down, brought down by demand, by the downright need for access to creative, cultural expression. More and more, artist and audience are becoming one—for the greater cause of community and mutuality.

When I started my career as a poet, it was in an "ivory tower" of a college campus. (Looking back, I can see that I was already trying to break down, overcome, transcend perceived barriers—because my first "official college" poem was dedicated to one of my West Side literary mentors, Charlie Parker.) Thus, not only was I in an isolated situation, I was also alone—as a "first" and an "only"—with ideas of somehow functioning in the "literary world."

I suppose if I had been a better bassist, or taken it up earlier, I would have opted for the jazz world—but being a jazz musician can also mean to function in obscurity and isolation. So poetry it was; it was something I could do, was even destined to do—since my mother, a teacher, had trained me in poetry since infancy. She read, I recited—for my grandparents, whomever; and when I started to read, she got books to me—even in camp, she somehow got me books: Robert Browning, Robert Louis Stevenson, Walter de la Mare . . . Thus, when I came home from college one day to announce, "I'm going to be a poet," my father said, "What's for supper?" (My parents were *relieved,* actually, that I was going to be *anything* other than irresponsible. They also knew that, as with my poetry teacher, Phil Levine, the teaching profession would come with the territory. Unless, heaven forbid, I were to become a "bohemian" poet—and we didn't come through the camps for that!)

Then an interesting thing happened while I was poetrying about from coast to coast in various campus "conservatories", publishing in the privacy of obscurity: History. The Sixties hit with a flash. Energy. Consciousness. Awareness. Empowerment and access. Groups grouped, movements moved. Flourished, nourished. Voices voiced. Cognition, recognition of what we already had, and how the world really is: the international planet of cultural plurality.

So you might say, "overnight," I began functioning as a *community poet*—with new people, places, and publications to work with. And it's a *privilege*, actually, to be asked to contribute, share, collaborate, participate, and to be granted a *functional, responsible* role in society.

And as my role expanded, my creativity had to develop and respond accordingly, to where it is now—at home in any context. When asked, I've served as a children's storyteller, a new spaper columnist, and a performer in any medium or setting—including public schools, churches, and community agencies. From the White House to the inner city—I've been there, *Ready*.

Thus, while most of the poems in this book have been presented in public (my favorite form of "publishing"—live, in the bardic and jazz traditions), all the poems in this section were written specifically for *performance*:

1. "Poems in Stone": These are "rock poems," performed by "The Standing Stones" of the Japanese American Historical Plaza, part of Tom McCall Waterfront Park, Portland, Oregon. The landscape architect, Robert Murase, asked me to contribute some poetry that would somehow convey the scope and sweep of our Oregon history—while also fitting in with his overall design. We hit upon the idea of creating "talking stones"—mini-poems in the haiku tradition, inscribed in stone, and set in chronological order, flowing with the flow of the Willamette River. These poems are like "voices" to be heard, to accompany and enhance, not distract from, a stroll through the wonderful setting. I created some "voices," and also selected some "voicings" from my accomplished elder, the late Mrs. Shizue Iwatsuki of Hood River. She was a remarkable person—a farming pioneer, wife and mother, who came to this country in 1916, and who was interned in Pinedale Camp (outside Fresno), Tule Lake Camp (California), and Minidoka Camp (Idaho). She was also a published poet in the Japanese tradition (these translations are by Professor Stephen Kohl of the University of Oregon), and she received a special emperor's award for her poetry in 1974. (Our combined poetry has inspired a major orchestral composition, *The American Nikkei Symphony*, by the great American pianist and composer, Andrew Hill. And, fittingly enough, when I was a child in camp, Andrew was a child in Chicago—a protégé of Earl "Fatha" Hines.)

2. "Akatonbo Song": Classical clarinetist Miles Ishigaki, a music professor at Fresno State, asked me to appear with him in concert, to benefit the Central California Nikkei Foundation. He sent me a suite of songs to work with—Japanese folk songs—and I responded with this poem, which we performed together. Since the occasion was for the community, with children and elders in attendance, and since the melodies are so sweet and gentle, I wanted to create something special, for everyone to relate to and enjoy. It was a beautiful evening, with a traditional, old country feeling.

3. "Headwaters": This poem was commissioned by the Actors' Theater, Ashland, for a fund-raising benefit. It was performed as a duo, with John Mazzei on keyboard synthesizer, while I moved about onstage—representing the journey from Ashland, over the Siskiyous, down past Mount Shasta, and on to the headwaters of the Sacramento River. There is also a progression through various "headwaters," from anxiety mind, to media mind, to academic mind, to memory mind, to just plain mind and life—or, from "uh oh" to "daijobu," which means "all right" in Japanese.

4. "Poem for Television": You never know who's watching. I wrote this poem for airing over our regional PBS affiliate. Who is that man? What is he talking about?

5. "On Being Asian American," and

6. "Something Grand": These poems were created for performances on college campuses, particularly for events sponsored by Asian American Studies Programs and Asian/Pacific Islander Student Unions. A poet can also be a minister, as an audience can also be a congregation, so these poems have employed a choir, a chorus, as well as a call-and-response effect; and, yes, of course, available music. ("Something Grand" was also presented at the White House, in 1980.)

7. "In The Stillness": This poem is not my own; most of the words are by someone else; I'm just the arranger. The real poet here is my teacher, the Venerable Lama Chhoje Rinpoche, founder of Padma Shedrup Ling, a Tibetan Buddhist spiritual center in Fairfax, California. I had been attending a week-long retreat of his teachings and, as

part of our concluding ceremonies, was asked to recite a poem. Natu-
rally, for that occasion, I simply drew upon his words from my notes,
arranging them into a poem: "*Thank you, Rinpoche.*"

8. "Red Earth, Blue Sky, Petrified": Finally, I want to close this book
with a "weaving." I attended an exhibit at the Denver Art Museum,
"Reflections of the Weaver's World," devoted to contemporary Navajo
weaving, and was simply humbled by the experience. Most of the
weavers are women, and many of them start from scratch, from the
earth itself—raising sheep, spinning yarn, making dyes from rocks and
plants. And then they sit there, "at prayer" before the loom, meditating
on and creating beauty—strand by strand, a beauty that truly "looms,"
I could never do that; I don't have their vision, skills, patience, context.
Still, in my own modest way, and with my own traditions at hand, I'm
a weaver of words. Perhaps I'm even a shepherd of sorts. Whatever, in
tribute to the people and their art, I wove this poem—word by word
and line by line, from my own materials, gathered and spun from the
workings of my life.

Mary Lee Begay: "When you set up the loom, you must measure care-
fully to the middle." Irene Clark: "Weaving's got some songs, good
songs, in it. You don't mess around with a rug."

Poems in Stone

THE JAPANESE AMERICAN HISTORICAL PLAZA, PORTLAND, OREGON

Mighty Willamette!
Beautiful friend,
I am learning,
I am practicing
To say your name.

Sure, I go to school
Same as you,
I'm an American.

Who? What?
When? Where?
Why?

Rounded up
In the sweltering yard.
Unable to endure any longer
Standing in line
Some collapse.
                    —Shizue Iwatsuki

Black smoke rolls
Across the blue sky.
Winter chills our bones.
This is Minidoka.
                         —Iwatsuki/Inada

Our young men and women
Joined the army, too.
They are proud to be American.

Going home,
Feeling cheated,
Gripping my daughter's hand,
I tell her we're leaving
Without emotion.
                              —Iwatsuki

Through the car window
A glimpse of pines.
Oregon mountains.
My heart beats faster,
Returning home.
                     —Iwatsuki

Glancing up
At red-tinged mountains,
My heart is softened.
A day in deep autumn.
                     —Iwatsuki

War and change,
My native land,
Once so hard to leave
Is behind me now
        forever.
                     —Iwatsuki

With new hope,
We build new lives.
Why complain when it rains?
This is what it means to be free.

Just over there
Was our old community.
Echoes! Echoes! Echoes!

Akatonbo Song

Akatonbo, red dragon fly—
where are you going?

Akatonbo, red dragon fly—
where are you going?

Akatonbo, red dragon fly—
where are you going?

    Akatonbo, red dragonfly—
    take me with you.

    Akatonbo, red dragonfly—
    take me with you.

    Akatonbo, red dragonfly—
    take me with you.

Let me ride the wind
with wings of music.

Let me ride the wind
with wings of music.

Let me ride the wind
with wings of music.

    Fly, dragon, fly!
    Fly, dragon, fly!
    Fly, dragon, fly!

Listen, Akatonbo—
a woman is singing.

Listen, Akatonbo—
a woman is singing.

    Look, Akatonbo—
    in these blue mountains.

    Look, Akatonbo—
    in these blue mountains.

    Look, Akatonbo—
    a woman is picking flowers.

Let us sing, too, Akatonbo!
Let us sing, too, Akatonbo!

    Let us bloom, too, Akatonbo!
    Let us bloom, too, Akatonbo!

Flowers of many colors!
Flowers of many colors!

    Red dragonfly, blue mountains!
    Red dragonfly, blue mountains!

White snow in the peaks!
White clouds in the sky!

White snow in the peaks!
White clouds in the sky!

    Listen, Akatonbo!
    Look, Akatonbo!

Blue, green, dream!

Listen, Akatonbo!
Look, Akatonbo!

Blue, green, dream!

III. KOKO NO SACHI ARI

And now it starts to rain, Akatonbo.
And now it starts to rain.

Here, Akatonbo—
come under this tree.

Here, Akatonbo—
come under this tree.

    Let it rain, Akatonbo!
    Let it rain!

    Such is life, Akatonbo!
    Such is life!

    The water of life!
    The water of life!

Already, on the horizon,
a golden sky!

Already, on the horizon,
a golden sky!

IV. UE WO MULTE ARU KOO

Sunset comes,
and a gentle evening.

Sunset comes,
and a gentle evening.

> My sleeves are wet, Akatonbo,
> and your wings are shining.

> My sleeves are wet, Akatonbo,
> and your wings are shining.

Far off, below,
the fields are shining.

Far off, below,
the fields are shining.

Far off, below,
the river is winding.

Far off, below,
the river is winding.

> A warm breeze blows, Akatonbo,
> A warm breeze blows.

Far off, below,
the village is shining.

Far off, below,
the village is shining.

> Let us go, Akatonbo!
> Let us go!

> Fly, dragonfly, fly!
> Fly, dragonfly, fly!

Sweet smoke in the village.
A star in the sky.

Sweet smoke in the village.
A star in the sky.

> Children are playing, Akatonbo.
> Children are playing.

> Women are singing, Akatonbo.
> Women are singing.

> Men are laughing, Akatonbo.
> Men are laughing.

> The food is cooking, Akatonbo.
> The food is cooking.

Sweet smoke in the village.
A star in the sky.

Sweet smoke in the village.
A star in the sky.

> Such is the life, Akatonbo.
> Such is the life.

VI. KIMI TO ITSU MADEMO

The stars sing, Akatonbo.
The stars sing.

Crickets shine, Akatonbo.
Crickets shine.

Souls sigh, Akatonbo.
Souls sigh.

    Lullaby, lullaby, lullaby, Akatonbo.
    Lullaby, lullaby, lullaby, Akatonbo.

Let me ride your wings, Akatonbo!
Let me ride your wings!

Let me ride your spirit, Akatonbo!
Let me ride your spirit!

Let us float through the sky, Akatonbo!
Let us float through the sky!

Let us float through our dreams, Akatonbo!
Let us float through our dreams!

    Goodnight, Akatombo!
    Goodnight!

Goodnight, Akatonbo!
Goodnight!

Headwaters

for John Mazzei

Headwaters
of the Sacramento,
just below
Shasta, brimming,
throbbing, overflowing
with images
from the journey
to the now:

traffic in the passes,
ascending, descending,
valleys, fields,
shining, light,
forests full of shadows—

quick, slow, close,
an expanse of distances . . .

Headwaters
of the Sacramento,
just below
Shasta, brimming,
throbbing, overflowing
with frequencies
from the journey
to the now:

"Hold on to your hats!
Here's 'Runaway Train'
by Roseann Cash . . ."

"Over on the coast it's . . . "

"That's right—it was
a dysfunctional family
with addictive personalities . . ."

Headwaters
of the Sacramento,
just below
Shasta, brimming,
throbbing, overflowing
with messages
from the past:

"Initially, we called them
Diggers, because they
dug roots for food,
but they also utilized
fish, game, berries,
and acorns like these,
grinding them into meal
on rocks like these—
see, see, you can still see
all the holes they left . . ."

"The Sierras came into being
during the Jurassic period:
the first conifers, the first
birds also appeared; this rock
is obviously sedimentary,
whereas when you read
the strata, you can see
metamorphic, igneous,
and so on down to the valley
and the alluvial plain . . ."

Headwaters
of the Sacramento,
just below
Shasta, here,

on this warm, smooth
rock still warm
from the sun, smooth
as a body sloping,
holding me, here,
I just want to be
here, holding my own
at the edge of water,
in this darkening canyon
in the gathering dusk:

yes, of course, of course,
I remember, remember:

    we had been up and down
    the North Fork without
    much luck, but had saved
    this favorite place for last:

    it was a tradition, since
    my father had landed that
    fabled rainbow just about
    dusk, so Uncle Min was
    heading out there on that
    rock when suddenly he
    shouted and then laughed;

    sure enough, that same
    old rattler had been
    sunning himself, and just
    now was disappearing
    into a crack; we laughed,
    and went on fishing;
    we all felt blessed
    just to be there; it was
    all *daijobu, daijobu* now . . .

Headwaters
of the Sacramento,
just below
Shasta, here,
I just want to be
here, incandescent
sunset on the ridges
silhouetting conifers,
I just want to be
here, on this rock,
listening to the river,
the incantations,
dipping my hands into
the glistening water,
raising the water
to my face, my eyes,
feeling the water,
knowing the water,
watching the droplets,
feeling the droplets
fall, and run, and dry;

I just want to be
here, on this rock,
watching the sky;

I just want to be
here, among the spirits,
when the full moon,
the first stars, appear;

my only ambition,
my only plan of action,
is to see the sun rise!

Headwaters

Sacrament

Images

Passes

Light

Shadows

Distances

Headwaters

Throbbing

Frequencies

Journey

Headwaters

Acorns

Conifers

Sedimentary

Metamorphic

Igneous

Headwaters

Smooth

Alluvial

Sloping

Holding

Gathering

Headwaters

Remember

Tradition

Rainbow

Blessing

Daijobu

Headwaters

Incandescent

Incantations

Glistening

Headwaters

Listening

Watching

Feeling

Knowing

Headwaters

Spirits

Rise

Poem for Television

Welcome to my poem.
Welcome to my home.

This is my song, my story,
this is my tell-a-vision
to you,

Listen! Can you hear me?
Look! Can you see me?

Yes! Yes!

As you experience
my being,
I am experiencing *you*.

What a wonder
this life is!

Look, listen—
around you!
Feel what is—
surrounds you!

And here I am,
and here you are,
and here we are—

maintaining,
retaining,
sustaining

our collective
community of humanity.

Is anything missing?
Is anything lacking?
Do we have enough stars?
Is one sun,
one moon,
one galaxy
enough for us?

Do we have enough crickets?
Do we have enough fish?
Do we have enough words?
Do we have enough music?
Do we have enough love?
Do we have enough spirit?

Think about it.
Think about it.

Tell about it.
Tell about it.

Celebrate your share.
Celebrate your share.

And in the celebration,
in the sharing,

we abide
with the wide sky
and the warm earth
of wisdom,

with the reverence
of ancestry,
with the reverence
of legacy,
with the reverence
of memory,
of history,

with the reverence
of benevolent
possibility

offered to us

in the dominion
of forests, rivers,
mountains, fields,

in the dominion
of oceans, seas,

in the dominion
of vast valleys,
of vast plateaus,
of vast expanses
of lands
of sun and rain and snow

where things are growing,
where things are being,
where everything has always been,
where everything will always be—
like children, singing.

The most interesting thing
about me

Is *you!*

On Being Asian American

for our children

Of course, not everyone
can be an Asian American.
Distinctions are earned,
and deserve dedication.

Thus, from time of birth,
the journey awaits you—
ventures through time,
the turns of the earth.

When you seem to arrive,
the journey continues;
when you seem to arrive,
the journey continues.

Take me as I am, you cry,
I, I, am an individual.
Which certainly is true.
Which generates an echo.

Who are all your people
assembled in celebration,
with wisdom and strength,
to which you are entitled.

For you are at the head
of succeeding generations,
as the rest of the world
comes forward to greet you.

As the rest of the world
comes forward to greet you.

Something Grand

CHANT FOR MANY VOICES

>From everywhere,
>We gather on this ground.
>From everywhere,
>We gather on this ground.
>
>From everywhere
>Let our spirits sound.
>From everywhere,
>Let our spirits sound.

Something grand.

Rain.
Sacred.

Something grand.

Sand.
Sacred.

Something grand.

Hands.
Sacred.

Something grand.

Stand.
Sacred.

Something grand.

Radiating.

Something grand.

Shaping.
Gracing.

Something grand.

Listen.

Something grand.

Listen.

Something grand.

We say
we are
that people.

Something grand.

Come down
through time
among peripheries.

Something grand.

Amazing
our selves
with song.

Something grand.

Strong things
spring
from our feet.

Something grand.

With wings.
With messages.

Something grand.

Listen. Listening.

Something grand.

Everything
we have
is this.

Something grand.

Everything
we have.

Something grand.

Is this.

Something grand.

Radiant.
Radiating.

Something grand.

Standing.
Dancing
in a field
after rain.

Something grand.

Standing.
Dancing

in the sunlight
after rain.

Something grand.

Something.

Something grand.

Something.

Something grand.

Something.

Something grand.

Something.

Something grand.

Something.

Something grand.

In the Stillness

for the Venerable Lama Chhoje Rinpoche

Lightning arises

In the stillness

A wave arises

In the stillness

A snake unwinds

In the stillness

The fountain freezes

In the stillness

The fountain flows

In the stillness

Dogs are warm

In the stillness

Form is emptiness

In the stillness

Emptiness is form

In the stillness

Watchful awareness

In the stillness

Realize the essence

In the stillness

Dharma is blameless

In the stillness

Dedicate the merit

In the stillness

Thank you, Rinpoche

In the stillness

Red Earth, Blue Sky, Petrified

A soft melody, over and over.
Red earth, blue sky, petrified.
Something shared by kindred spirits.
Common as clay, regular as rain.
It simply comes with the territory.
Dusk. Little summer breeze.
Full moon rising. Stars.
Birds, insects. Juniper, sage.
Something about who and how we are.
History and destiny. Character.
The whole prophecy. We are not alone.

*

Aspects of humanity, the human condition
The purpose of uniting. Services. Respect.
Responsible. Sufficient. Essential. Effects.
Securely. Plainly. Numbered. Accordance.
Kind. Personal. Substantial. Accepted.
Given. Let us bring. Let us have.
Friends, neighbors, colleagues, partners.
Fields and places. Society and commerce.
Rainbows. Freedom of choice, options.
Spirits. Land. Dreams. Visions.
Sand. Creek. Moon. Black. Red.
Denver. Sacramento. Hiroshima.
Battle. Creek. America. Planets.
Marysville, Placerville, Watsonville.
The blue tricycle left in the weeds.
Bridge. Lights. Long since passed.
Chanting, droning. Persistent, specific.
Shooting. Shouting. Shot. Missed.
Buddha. Buddhas. Down the rows, rows, rows.
Calligraphy of echoes. At Amache Gate.
Sit. Listen. Love. Sing. Concentrate.

*

Ancestry. Family. People of the land.
Home. The pattern of survival.

Continues. Remains. In full force.
Vineyards. Cottonfields. Deep.
South. Northern. West. Resources.
Above. Beneath. The spirit thrives.
In the marketplace. Lima. Fresnillo.
Zimbabwe. Through the music. Heat.
Around and around. Around and around.
Ocean. Continents. F Street.
Walk along the Ganges. Wade. Recite.
Whales, polar bears, seals. Tundra.
Dirt. Good. Dirt. Good. Gardens.
Tomatoes, squash, peppers, corn.
Orange. Tree. Cactus. Living.
Life in the valleys and mountains.
Mama. Sweet. Moths. Fluttering.
Earth. Spheres. World. Farmers.
Center. In the glory of it. Glowing.
In the radiance. Our songs, our songs.
Love, fun, animals, and valor. Lands.
Languages. Voices. Praise. Aspire.
To the very heart. Entrusted. Trusted.
Cup coffee, piece pie. Come today fresh.
Common concepts of collective survival.
                    *

Warm. Gentle. Soothing. Special.
Bright and red and yellow and shiny.
Dance and sing. Mood. Indigo.
Sand. Dusk. Stars. Whistle.
A path, a way, a vision, a direction.
Humor. Wisdom. Power. Beauty.
Functional. Functioning. Equally.
Love. Life. Music. Gift.
Common. Colored. Community.
                    *

A soft melody, over and over.
Red earth, blue sky, petrified.